THE CHANGING WORLD

EARTHQUAKES & VOLCANOES

JOHN STIDWORTHY

THUNDER BAY
P·R·E·S·S

Code of Safety

All activities should be conducted under adult supervision. Most of the habitats described in this series are dangerous because they are at the extremes of how our world works. They are not places you should visit without preparation or without a qualified guide. You should take suitable equipment and wear the right clothing for the environment. Take a map and a compass on all trips and learn how to use them properly. If you should find yourself in such a place through an accident, you will find some tips on how to survive there on page 67.

- **Before you go on a trip**, plan your route. **Always** tell an adult where you are going and when you expect to return.
- **Always go with a friend**, and preferably go as a party of four, which is a safe minimum number.

  If possible, go with at least one adult whom you trust—ideally someone who knows the area and the subject you are studying.
- **Ask permission** before going on to private property.
- **Leave gates closed or open** depending on how you find them. Keep off crops and avoid damaging soils, plants, animals, fences, walls, and gates.
- **Take your litter home** or dispose of it properly.
- **Remember** that many plants and animals, and their homes and habitats, are protected by law.
- **Ask your parents** not to light fires except in an emergency.
- **Beware of natural hazards** such as slippery slopes, crumbling cliffs, loose rocks, rotten tree trunks and branches, soft mud, deep water, swift currents, and tides.
- **Beware of poisonous berries**, plants, and animals: if you are not sure, don't touch them.
- Remember: **if in doubt, always play safe.**

Picture Credits

Susanna Addario: 64/65. Bruce Coleman Ltd: 24 (Gunter Ziesler); 46/47 (Kim Taylor). Peter Bull: 16/17; 20/21; 24/25; 28/29; 38/39; 46/47. Frank Spooner Pictures: 57. The Hutchison Library: 43 (Macintyre). Rex Features: 7; 27. Robert Harding Picture Library: 42. Mike Saunders: 6/7; 11; 12/13; 18/19; 22/23; 32/33; 56/57; 66. Science Photo Library: 36 (Roger Ressmeyer, Starlight); back cover, endpapers, 1 (© Tom Van Sant, Geosphere Project, Santa Monica). Michael Shoebridge: 30/31; 37; 43; 52. Ed Stewart: 10/11. Tim Thackeray: 53; 54/55; 58/59; 62/63. Gerald Witcomb, Specs Art: 8/9; 26; 34/35; 36; 40/41; 42; 44/45; 48/49; 50/51. Activity pictures by Mr Gay Galsworthy.

Thunder Bay Press
5880 Oberlin Drive, Suite 400
San Diego, CA 92121

First published in the United States and Canada by Thunder Bay Press, 1996

Editor	Diana Briscoe
Series Editor	Steve Parker
Designer	Martyn Foote
Art Director	John Strange
Design Assistants	Karen Ferguson
	Victoria Furbisher
DTP Manager	Michael Burgess
Editorial Director	Pippa Rubinstein

Library of Congress Cataloging-in-Publication Data
Stidworthy, John, 1943–
   Earthquakes & volcanoes / [text, John Stidworthy.]
   p.   cm. — (The changing world)
   Includes index.
   Summary: Looks at some of the visible ways that the earth can be changed in a matter of minutes, and discusses how the natural forces involved in earthquakes and volcanoes can raise mountains, build islands, change weather, and help to produce varieties of plants and animals.
   ISBN 1–57145–124–2
   1. Earthquakes—Juvenile literature.
   2. Volcanoes—Juvenile literature.
   [1. Earthquakes.   2. Volcanoes.]
I. Title   II. Series: Changing world (San Diego, Calif.)
QE521.3.S75   1996
551.2—dc20
                                         96–5008
                                              CIP
                                               AC

Typeset by Dragon's World Ltd in Garamond, Caslon 540 and Frutiger.
Printed in Italy

Contents

The Changing World of
Earthquakes and Volcanoes

Our world, planet Earth, has never been still since it first formed—4,600 million years ago. It goes around the Sun once each year, to bring the changing seasons. It spins like a top once each day, causing the cycle of day and night. Our close companion, the Moon, circles the Earth and produces the rise and fall of the ocean tides. The weather alters endlessly, too. Winds blow, water ripples into waves, clouds drift, rain falls, and storms brew. Land and sea are heated daily by the Sun, and cool or freeze at night.

Living on the Earth, we notice these changes on different time scales. First and fastest is our own experience of passing time, as seconds merge into minutes and hours. We move about, eat and drink, learn and play, rest and sleep. Animals do many of these activities, too.

Second is the longer, slower time scale of months and years. Many plants grow and change over these longer time periods. Return to a natural place after many years, and you see how some of the trees have grown, while others have died and disappeared.

Third is the very long, very slow time scale lasting hundreds, thousands, and millions of years. The Earth itself changes over these immense periods. New mountains thrust up as others wear down. Rivers alter their course. One sea fills with sediments, but huge earth movements and continental drift create another sea elsewhere.

The *CHANGING WORLD* series describes and explains these events—from the immense time span of lands and oceans, to the shorter changes among trees and flowers, to the daily lives of ourselves and other animals. Each book selects one feature or habitat of nature, to reveal in detail. Here you can read how *EARTHQUAKES AND VOLCANOES* unleash their awesome power in a few seconds, when they change the landscape over hundreds or thousands of miles, create new islands and mountains, and provide different habitats for plants and animals.

MORE, AND MORE, AND ...

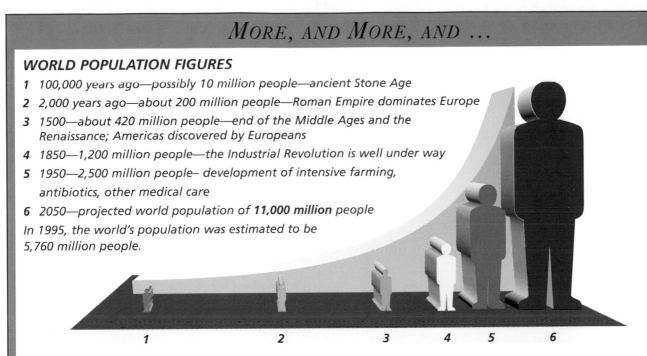

WORLD POPULATION FIGURES

1 100,000 years ago—possibly 10 million people—ancient Stone Age

2 2,000 years ago—about 200 million people—Roman Empire dominates Europe

3 1500—about 420 million people—end of the Middle Ages and the Renaissance; Americas discovered by Europeans

4 1850—1,200 million people—the Industrial Revolution is well under way

5 1950—2,500 million people– development of intensive farming, antibiotics, other medical care

*6 2050—projected world population of **11,000 million** people*

In 1995, the world's population was estimated to be 5,760 million people.

The most numerous large animal on Earth, by many millions, is the human. Our numbers have increased steadily from the start of civilization about 10,000 years ago, speeded by advances in public health and hygiene, the Industrial Revolution, gas and diesel engines, better farming, and better medical care.

However, this massive growth in humanity means that almost half the world's people suffer from hunger, poverty, and disease. The animals and plants who share our planet also suffer. As we expand our territory, their natural areas shrink ever faster. We probably destroy one species of plant or animal every week.

However, there is another type of change affecting our world. It is the huge and ever-increasing number of humans on the planet. The CHANGING WORLD series shows how we have completely altered vast areas—to grow foods, put up homes and other buildings, mine metals and minerals, manufacture goods and gadgets from pencils to washing machines, travel in cars, trains and planes, and generally live in our modern world.

This type of change is causing immense damage.

We take over natural lands and wild places, forcing plants and animals into ever-smaller areas. Some of them disappear for ever. We produce all kinds of garbage, waste, poisons water and air pollution.

However, there is hope. More people are becoming aware of the problems. They want to stop the damage, to save our planet, and to plan for a brighter future. The CHANGING WORLD series shows how we can all help. We owe it to our Earth, and to its millions of plants, animals and other living things, to make a change for the better.

The Power of Nature

Volcanic eruptions and earthquakes have massive power, far beyond anything that people can imagine. Every few years there is new devastation. In June 1991, the volcano of Mount Pinatubo, Philippines, erupted. There were warning signs of rumbles and spurts of gas, which gave time for 200,000 people within 25 miles to move away. The huge energy of the explosive eruption shook the area and threw searing-hot ash 20 miles into the air.

In January 1995, when it was still dark and most people were asleep in bed, an earthquake shook the city of Kobe in Japan like a giant jello, for twenty seconds. Many buildings collapsed, killing their occupants. More than 5,000 people died, and at least 300,000 were made homeless.

Flee or die
The eruption of a volcano is one of the most awesome events in nature. Tons of lava, which is red-hot liquid rock, spurt out and flow over the land, burning everything in its path. Choking ashes are hurled into the air and settle, blanketing the landscape for many miles. All living things must flee—or die.

THE DANGER OF FIRE

Many newer, better-designed buildings survived the Kobe earthquake. But some modern structures, including hospitals and an elevated highway, were destroyed. Electricity cables and gas pipes broke, causing explosions and fires. In many earthquakes, the biggest danger is fire raging out of control. Firefighters cannot reach the area by road, and water pipes are broken. After Tokyo's 1923 quake, a firestorm killed more than 100,000 people.

Volcano and Quake Zones

In some parts of the world, earthquakes and volcanoes are extremely rare. They include Australia, northern Europe, eastern North America, and northern Asia. In contrast, some parts of the world are never free from the possibility of an earthquake or volcanic eruption, as shown below.

There are about 500 "active" volcanoes, which means they have erupted recently and may do so again at any time. The great majority of these lie on the "Ring of Fire" around the Pacific Ocean. This ring stretches along Japan and north-east Asia, across the Bering Straits to Alaska, down the Rocky

Eurasia and Africa
Iceland is full of volcanic action, sometimes low-key, sometimes violent. In Europe, southern Italy has several major volcanoes, including Vesuvius, Stromboli, Etna, and the island volcano that gave all others its name: Vulcano.

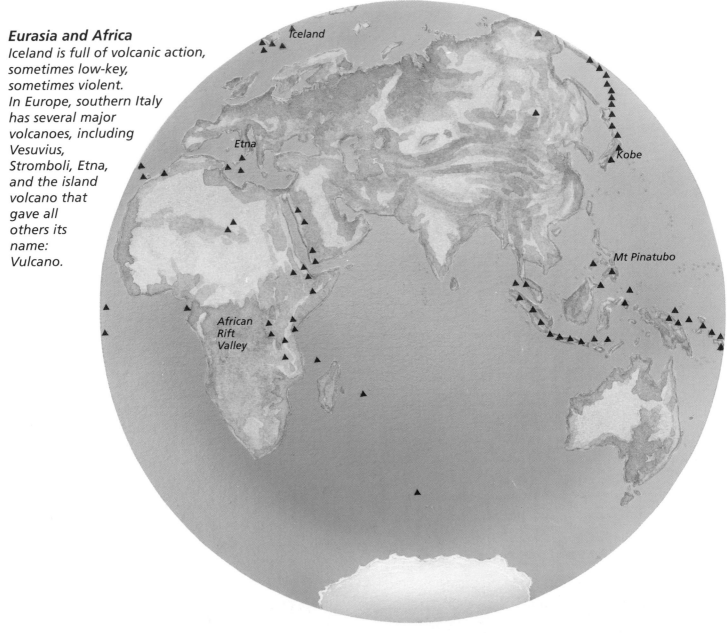

Iceland

Etna

Kobe

Mt Pinatubo

African Rift Valley

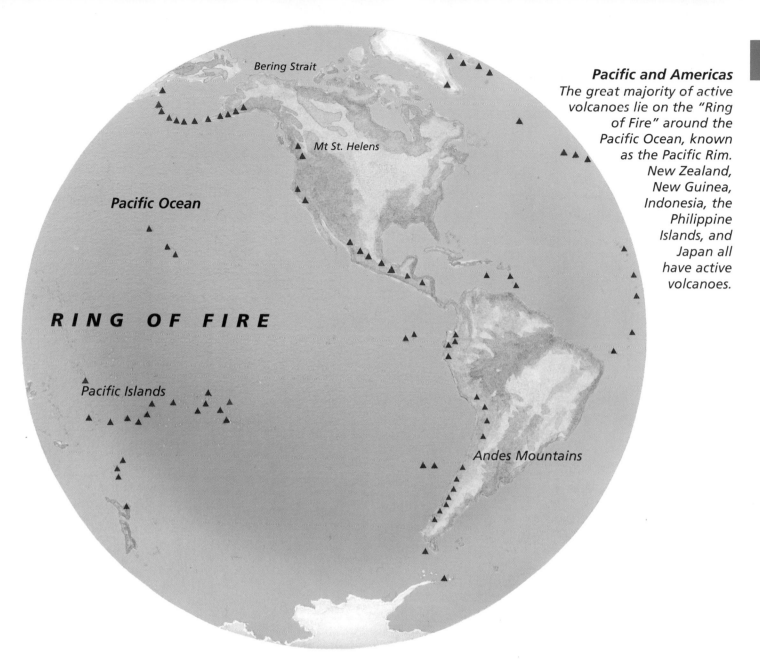

Bering Strait

Mt St. Helens

Pacific Ocean

RING OF FIRE

Pacific Islands

Andes Mountains

Pacific and Americas
The great majority of active volcanoes lie on the "Ring of Fire" around the Pacific Ocean, known as the Pacific Rim. New Zealand, New Guinea, Indonesia, the Philippine Islands, and Japan all have active volcanoes.

Mountains in the western USA (where Mount St. Helens exploded in 1980), and down through Central America into the Andes of South America.

The areas affected by earthquakes are much the same as those that have volcanoes. Many quakes happen at the edges of the continental landmasses. Some continental edges, as in California or China, have large populations that are at risk. However, North Africa and Central Asia have many earthquakes, but no volcanoes. There are also volcanoes and earthquakes under the sea. We rarely hear about these, unless an undersea quake sets off a tsunami (a huge wave), or a volcano builds itself high enough in the sea to form an island.

In an average year, scientists detect about 6,000 earthquakes. But most are so small, or in such remote places, that they are unnoticed. About 500 are felt by people. Of these, 30 to 40 cause serious damage. About ten earthquakes and five eruptions produce greater damage and make world news.

The Restless Earth

The Earth's outer skin, or crust, is not one continuous, rigid surface. It is made up of separate, gigantic, curved sheets of rock, like a cracked eggshell. The sheets are known as "tectonic plates." Some plates carry whole continents or parts of continents, such as North America and the shallow seas around it. Other plates form vast slabs of the ocean floor. Continental plates and oceanic plates are different in structure. The rocks in the oceanic plates are denser than those that make up the continental plates. However, the upper layer of an ocean plate, known as the oceanic crust, is only about 7 miles thick. The continental crust is thicker, at 20–30 miles.

Slowly, very slowly, the plates move. We do not usually notice this movement, but it can be measured. Western Europe is moving away from

Continental drift
The main landmasses of the world have travelled around the globe over millions of years. They ride piggyback on their great slabs of continental crust. Between them are much thinner plates of oceanic crust, which are being made in some areas and destroyed in others.

Into the Earth's core
The diagram on the right shows a cutaway view of the Earth. The outermost layer is the crust. It is formed from about 20 tectonic plates, which fit together like a ball-shaped jigsaw and slowly move about. In proportion to the whole Earth, the crust is very thin—thinner than the skin on an apple. Below the crust is the mantle, made up of molten rock and about 1,800 miles thick. Next is the outer core. This is probably made of molten iron and nickel, and is about 1,400 miles thick. In the center is the inner core, a solid ball of iron and nickel which is about 1,600 miles across. Its temperature is around 9,000° Fahrenheit (water boils at 212° Fahrenheit).

Today

50 million years ago

200 million years ago

Where plates meet
As shown on the right, an oceanic plate may slide under a thicker, less dense continental plate, whose edges buckle to form mountains. As the oceanic rocks are forced deeper, they melt and the molten rock rises through cracks to form a line of volcanoes. This is happening along the Andes Mountains in South America.

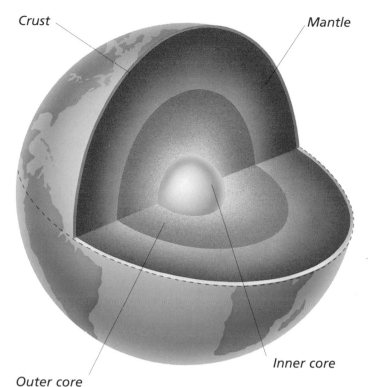

Crust

Mantle

Outer core

Inner core

eastern North America by 1 inch each year, as the Atlantic Ocean gets wider. But the world is not getting bigger overall. The edges of some plates are being squeezed together, while other plates are getting wider (see page 12.) The areas where plates are being crushed together, or where their edges are being enlarged, are the places where you find most volcanoes and earthquakes. This process has been going on almost since the Earth began. The result is that the Earth's landmasses have slowly wandered around its surface. We call it "continental drift."

How do we know? Scientists can trace similar rock layers and fossils in continents that are now widely separated. This suggests the continents were once joined. There is also evidence from the Earth's natural magnetism (see page 12.) And very accurate satellite methods can measure the drift, even a few millimetres per year, to show it's really happening.

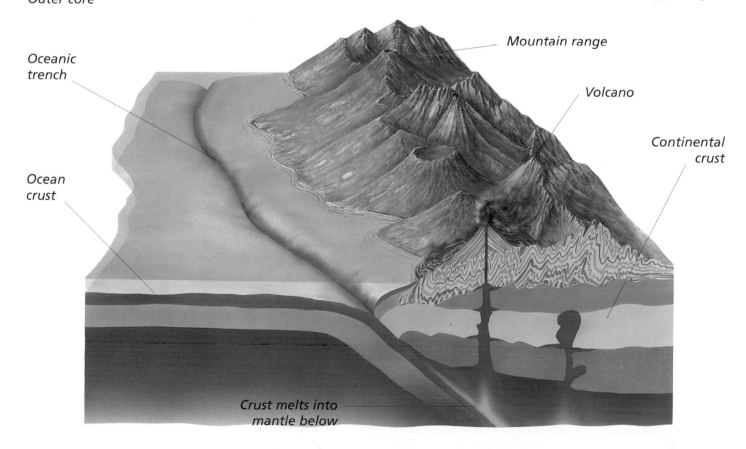

Oceanic trench

Ocean crust

Mountain range

Volcano

Continental crust

Crust melts into mantle below

Sea-floor Spreading

Midway across the Atlantic Ocean, deep on the seabed, incredibly hot liquid rock rises from deep in the Earth's interior. The molten rock spreads sideways as it nears the surface, pushing the plates apart. A crack develops between the plates. Molten rock rises through the crack and seeps out on to the ocean floor—like a long, thin, undersea volcano.

As the melted rock oozes up and meets the water, it cools and solidifies, adding to the edges of the sideways-moving plates. The result is a long ridge of mountains on the sea floor, with a crack running along its length. This process is called sea-floor spreading. It makes some plates bigger, but others get smaller where they melt back into the Earth.

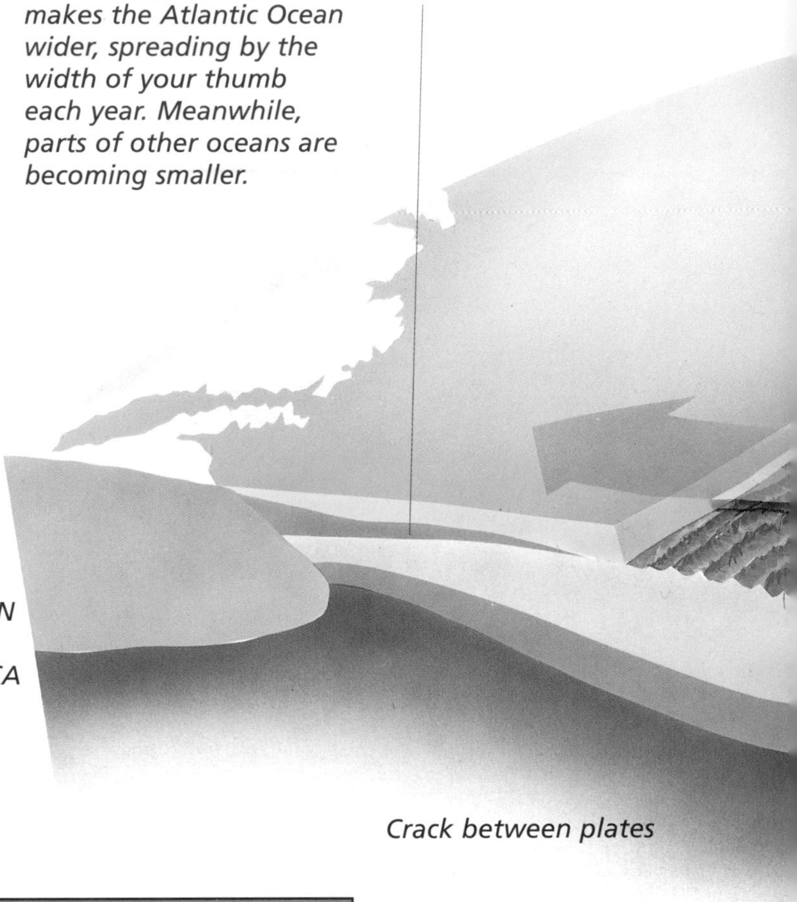

Sea-floor spreading
Almost continuous ridges of mountains run through the world's oceans, far beneath the water. Here new rock is made, and the plates grow as they slide sideways. In other places the plates crunch together and an edge is destroyed as it melts back deep into the Earth. This diagram shows the Mid-Atlantic Ridge.

The widening Atlantic
Sea-floor spreading makes the Atlantic Ocean wider, spreading by the width of your thumb each year. Meanwhile, parts of other oceans are becoming smaller.

Old sea-floor rock with lots of sediments

EASTERN
NORTH
AMERICA

Crack between plates

MAGNETIC CLUES

The Earth's magnetic field has flipped through time, the North Magnetic Pole switching to South and then back again—perhaps two or three times every million years. As certain rocks form, the direction of the Earth's magnetism is "frozen" into them, like millions of tiny compass needles. Moving out from the mid-oceanic ridges, the rocks contain "stripes" that record magnetism in alternate directions. They also show how the rocks get older, farther from the ridge.

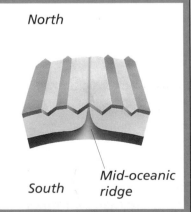

North

South

Mid-oceanic ridge

Sands of time
The new rock at the plate edge has no sand, mud, or other sediment on it, since it formed so recently. As it moves farther from the ridge, sand and mud gradually settle on it, in an ever-thickening blanket. The oldest rocks at the edge of the ocean may have 14,000 feet of sand and other sediments resting on top of them.

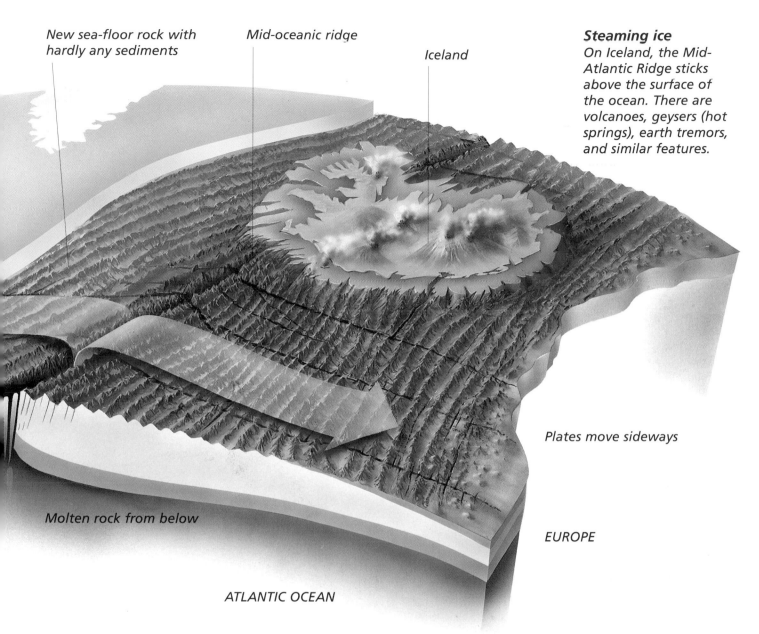

New sea-floor rock with hardly any sediments

Mid-oceanic ridge

Iceland

Steaming ice
On Iceland, the Mid-Atlantic Ridge sticks above the surface of the ocean. There are volcanoes, geysers (hot springs), earth tremors, and similar features.

Plates move sideways

Molten rock from below

EUROPE

ATLANTIC OCEAN

The Mid-Atlantic Ridge is just one part of a system of mid-oceanic ridges that stretches for 50,000 miles through the world's oceans. The ridges are generally in the middle of the oceans, but in the Pacific they are much closer to the edges, as shown on the previous pages. The underwater mountains of the ridge may be more than two miles higher than the surrounding sea floor.

Sea-floor spreading is basically volcanic, but it tends to be slow and regular, without the explosive outbursts of volcanoes on land. In some places the mountain peaks rise above the water's surface as islands, and the volcanoes erupt into the air. Iceland is such a place, on the northern end of the Mid-Atlantic Ridge. Tristan da Cunha and Ascension are other volcanic islands on the Mid-Atlantic Ridge.

Edible Lava Flow Fun

You can have some fun—messy fun—making Jello®, dessert toppings (like Cool Whip), and foods of similar kinds, and seeing how they flow, spread out and set. Different types of lava do the same. Use foods that need to be mixed or dissolved in a certain amount of water. Most of these desserts and pastes set by drying or chemical change, whereas lavas set by going cool and solid. But the main results are the same.

You need a selection of Jello®, dessert toppings, and similar foods, plus bowls and trays, and water. You could try the same idea with flour-and-water paste or a similar type of paste, but you MUST not eat this! NOTE You must have the help and advice of an adult when warming and using hot water.

1 Read the instructions on the packet, telling how to make the food in the normal way. Prepare a portion like this, for practice. An adult should heat the water before you stir in the powder or pieces. Note how runny it is before it sets.

3 See how the food runs and slides down the sides of the bowl, like lava oozing from a volcano. Does it form ripples and waves? Make a sketch in your notebook, showing the surface features of the "lava flow."

5 Make another portion, but use even less water, perhaps one quarter of the recommended amount. Is the food thicker and stiffer than before? Pour it over the bowl "volcano." Note the surface patterns that form, and see how far it flows.

6 You could make up several fairly thick, stiff portions, and build your own edible volcano! Pour the first one carefully into the center of a deep, flat plate. Let it spread and set. Do this several times, always pouring onto the center, in the same way that lava comes out of the same vent in a volcano. Try using food portions of different colors.

14

2 *Make up a small portion of the same food, but add only one half of the recommended amount of water, for the quantity you use. After mixing, pour it over the cleaned, upturned bowl, that you put on the cleaned tray.*

4 *How far does the food flow, and why does it stop? Does it spread itself out too thinly? Perhaps it begins to set, becoming too thick and stiff to flow any further. Different types of lava do this, building different shapes of volcanoes.*

7 *After several layers, you should have built up a dome or cone shape, like a real volcano. Now slice the edible version and see how the colored layers have piled on top of each other. They are like the layers of hardened rock lava in a proper volcano.*

Underwater Volcano

The deep-sea vents and "black smokers" on the ocean floor send plumes of molten rock, boiling fumes, superheated steam, particles, and chemicals from deep below into the surrounding water. You can show this by making an undersea volcano that erupts colored water instead of gases and lava. You need a piece of string, some food dye or coloring, a large, clear jar or bowl, a small, clear glass bottle that fits easily into the large jar or bowl, and some cold and warm water.

1 *Fill the large jar or bowl about three-quarters full with cold faucet water. Dip the small bottle into it, to check that you can put it in completely without the water overflowing.*

2 *Tie the string around the small bottle's neck so that you can lift it up safely. Put 5–10 drops of food coloring into the bottle.*

3 *Fill the rest of the small bottle with fairly warm water from the hot faucet. Be careful not to scald or burn yourself if the water is hot.*

4 *Now pick up the small bottle by the string, and lower it down into the water in the large jar or bowl. It should sink easily. Lower it to rest gently on the bottom.*

5 *Watch what happens. The hot water in the bottle rises like hot lava and gases from a deep-sea vent. You can see the water's movement because of the food coloring. It swirls up into the cold water, and the two gradually mix. It's an ocean-floor smoker!*

Under the Earth's hard outer crust is a vast layer of molten (melted) rock, called "magma." It is under enormous pressure and is squeezed up at any weak place in the crust, such as between tectonic plates. The magma may collect in a magma chamber or reservoir under the volcano, before rising through cracks or "pipes" to a hole on the surface. The result is a volcano.

When the magma reaches the surface, it becomes known as lava. Its temperature may be as high as 2,200° Fahrenheit. How the lava erupts depends on its temperature, thickness, and consistency, and the pressure down below, forcing it upwards. It may burst out like a fountain when this pressure is released. Some magma also contains lots of gases, under pressure. The pressure release at the surface means that the gases bubble and blow out high into the air, like taking the top off a shaken-up can of

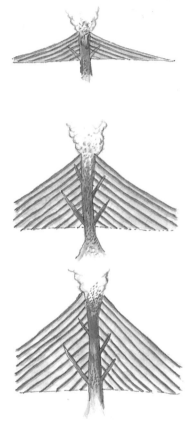

How a volcano grows
In a cone volcano, eruptions of sticky lava cool and solidify close to the vent. Layers of lava alternate with layers of ash from explosive eruptions, to build the steep-sided cone higher and higher. Rain may wear deep gullies in the slopes.

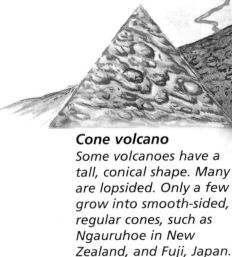

Cone volcano
Some volcanoes have a tall, conical shape. Many are lopsided. Only a few grow into smooth-sided, regular cones, such as Ngauruhoe in New Zealand, and Fuji, Japan.

soda. Or the lava may come out gently and run like a slow, thick river down the slopes of the volcano. If the lava is thin and runny, it may travel for many miles and reach speeds of 30 mph, faster than any human can run. However most lava is thicker and more soupy, so it flows slowly.

As soon as lava reaches the air, it begins to cool, back into solid rock. Fast-flowing lava may take on a ropy appearance, while thicker, stickier lava solidifies into rough, sharp blocks. Sometimes the lava on the surface cools and goes hard, but, just beneath, it is still hot enough to flow. If the eruption ends, the lower lava may flow away, leaving hollow caverns under the upper, hardened lava. Most lava flows are too slow to endanger people, but they engulf and destroy trees, buildings, farms, and anything else in their path.

In some places, huge outpourings of runny lava have flooded across the land, covering vast areas and hardening into almost flat sheets of rock. In western India over millions of years, lava outflows have spread over more than 19,300 square miles, forming the Deccan Plateau, with layers of volcanic rock 6,600 feet thick. There are similar lava floods in Australia, South Africa, Brazil, and the Columbia River area of the USA.

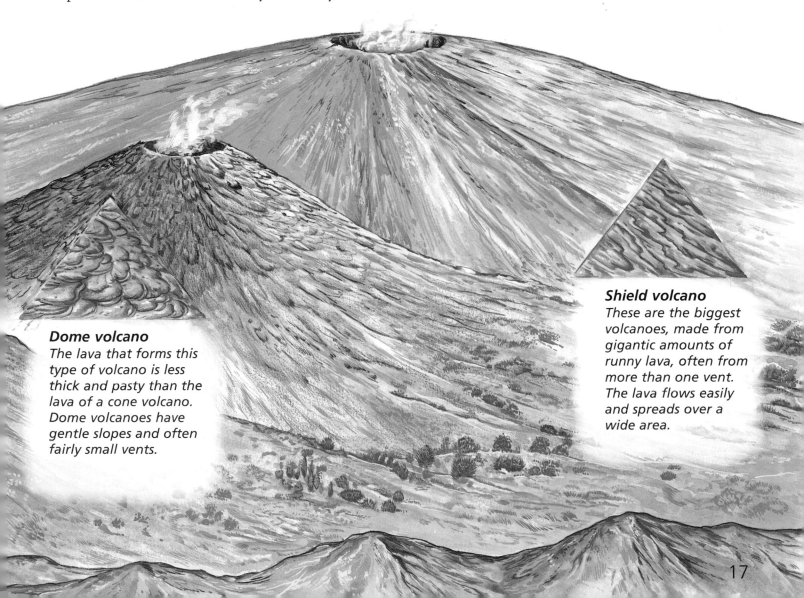

Dome volcano
The lava that forms this type of volcano is less thick and pasty than the lava of a cone volcano. Dome volcanoes have gentle slopes and often fairly small vents.

Shield volcano
These are the biggest volcanoes, made from gigantic amounts of runny lava, often from more than one vent. The lava flows easily and spreads over a wide area.

Beneath the Surface

When a volcano becomes dormant or "asleep," this means it is not active—but it could re-awaken and erupt any time. Despite the quiet surface, there may be lots of activity under the ground. If you could take away the surrounding rock from under a volcano, you would see how the magma has formed vast chambers, seeped along cracks, and found any other weak points in the complex layers of rock that make up the crust. The magma pushes its way under tremendous pressure, into and around the surrounding layers of rock, forcing them apart.

In some cases, the volcano never becomes active again. In effect, it dies, and is known as an extinct volcano. The magma under the surface cools and goes solid, too. It may form many different features, depending on how and where it flows, and how fast it cools. If the magma cools quickly, it becomes coarse-grained rock with large particles which you can easily see. One of the commonest examples is the very hard rock known as granite. Blocks of granite were used for castles and other long-lasting buildings. Slow-cooling magma forms rocks with very fine grains. The commonest example is basalt.

If the magma pushes into a long crack between the surrounding rock layers, and then goes solid and hard, this is called a dike. Sometimes the magma is forced into and through the nearby layers of rock. The resulting layer of hardened volcanic rock, which cuts across the surrounding rock layers, is called a sill. A batholith is a gigantic lump of magma that has formed a bulge in the crust and then become solid, without breaking the surface to form a volcano. These huge rock features may stay hidden beneath the surface for millions of years. Eventually, if the rock above is worn away or eroded, features such as dikes, sills, and batholiths are exposed at the surface.

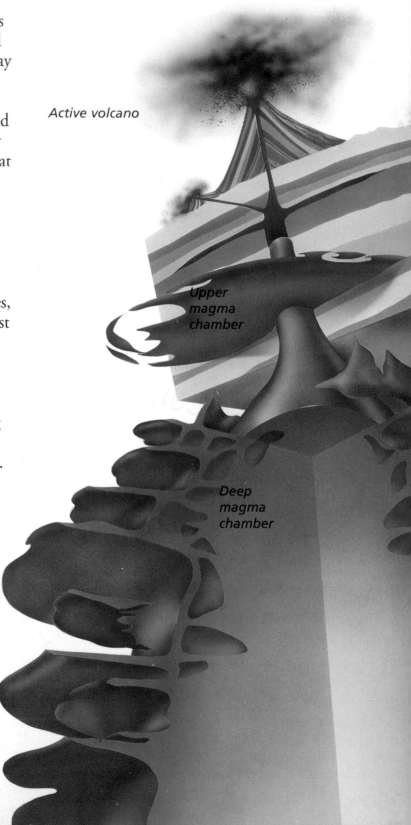

Active volcano

Upper magma chamber

Deep magma chamber

18

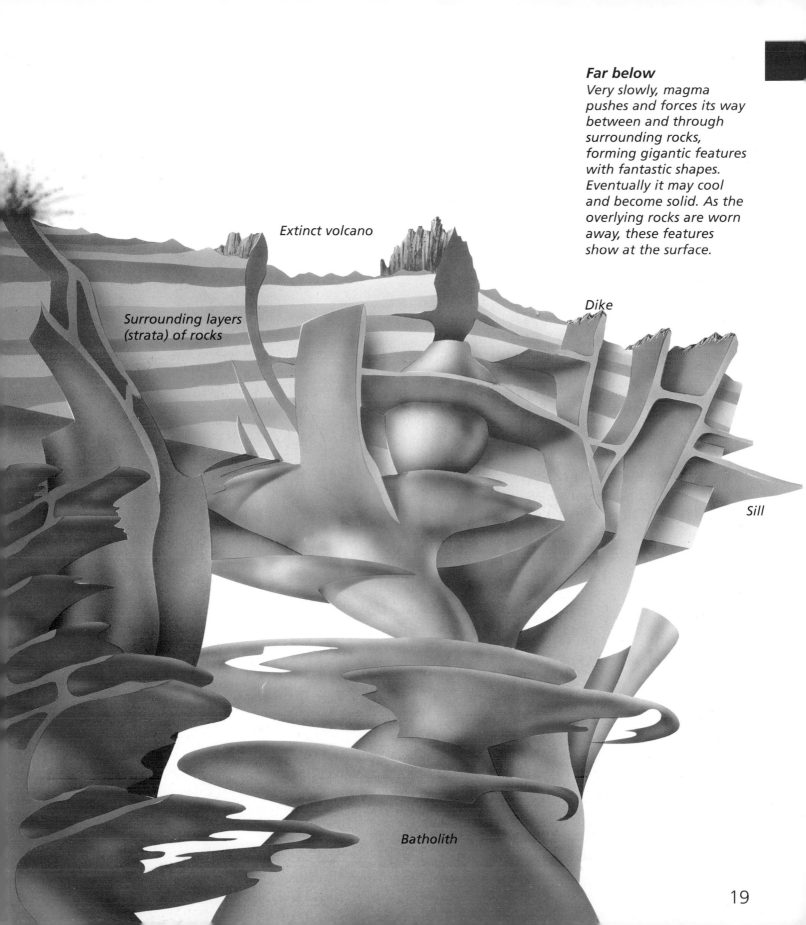

Far below
Very slowly, magma pushes and forces its way between and through surrounding rocks, forming gigantic features with fantastic shapes. Eventually it may cool and become solid. As the overlying rocks are worn away, these features show at the surface.

Extinct volcano

Surrounding layers (strata) of rocks

Dike

Sill

Batholith

What Volcanoes Spit Out

Not only lava comes out of a volcano. There are many other substances, which can ooze out slowly or be hurtled many miles, depending on the explosive power of the eruption. They include fine particles of ash, fumes, and gases, and various-sized lumps of rock known as volcanic bombs, which fly through the air like red-hot missiles.

When magma is very thick and full of gas, it may erupt explosively, sending a cloud of ash high into the air. Volcanic ash is not the remains of something burned, but a collection of fine lava and rock particles. It may blanket a huge area when it settles, darkening the sky so it is like night. The main clouds of gas and ash from volcanoes can carry a surprising distance, up to 125 miles.

When the volcano Mt. Saint Helens exploded in 1980, the main dark cloud of ash blew like a hurricane through an area 20 miles wide and 12 miles long. Winds may carry finer particles of ash much farther. Some of the volcanic ash from Mt Saint Helens settled on the Great Plains of North America—1,000 miles away.

Another major volcanic hazard is the mud flow, or lahar. Water mixes with volcanic ash to produce a very slippery slurry that can slide rapidly down a

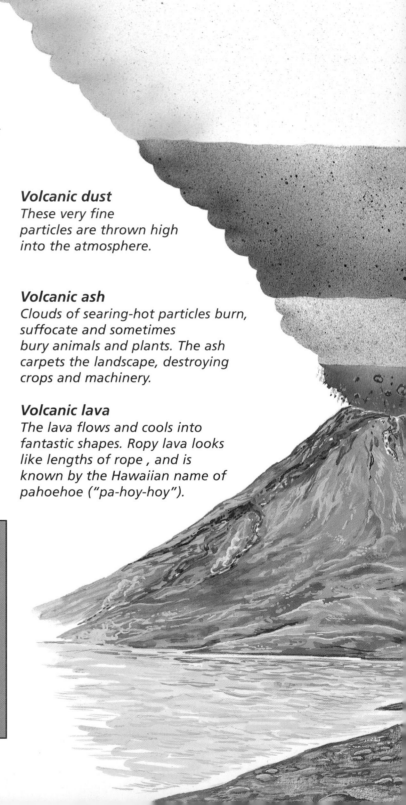

Volcanic dust
These very fine particles are thrown high into the atmosphere.

Volcanic ash
Clouds of searing-hot particles burn, suffocate and sometimes bury animals and plants. The ash carpets the landscape, destroying crops and machinery.

Volcanic lava
The lava flows and cools into fantastic shapes. Ropy lava looks like lengths of rope , and is known by the Hawaiian name of pahoehoe ("pa-hoy-hoy").

A ROCK THAT FLOATS

Sometimes lava is thrown from a volcano and cools with bubbles of gas still trapped in it, so that it is like a hardened sponge. This is pumice, a very light, honeycombed rock that can float on water.

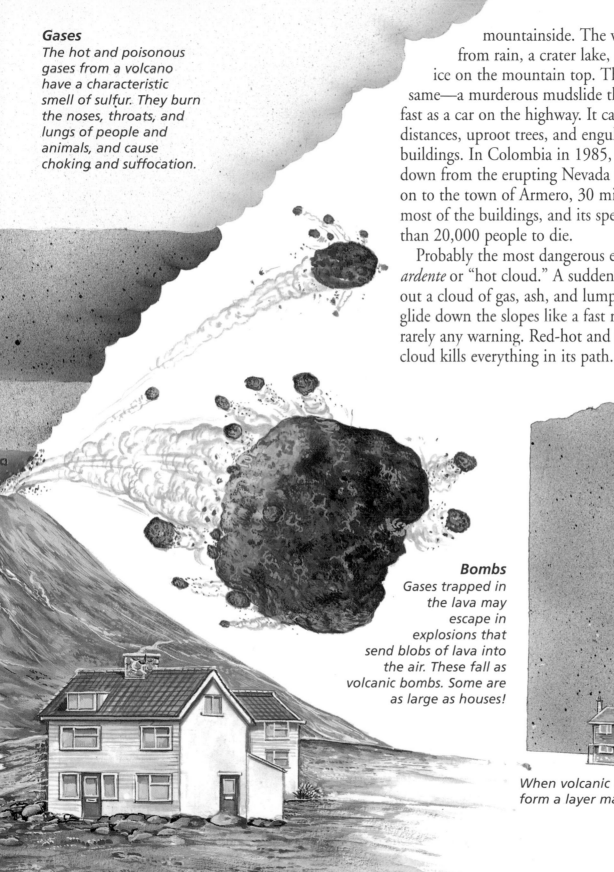

Gases

The hot and poisonous gases from a volcano have a characteristic smell of sulfur. They burn the noses, throats, and lungs of people and animals, and cause choking and suffocation.

mountainside. The water may come from rain, a crater lake, or melting snow or ice on the mountain top. The result is the same—a murderous mudslide that may move as fast as a car on the highway. It can travel huge distances, uproot trees, and engulf bridges and buildings. In Colombia in 1985, a lahar swept down from the erupting Nevada del Ruiz volcano on to the town of Armero, 30 miles away. It buried most of the buildings, and its speed caused more than 20,000 people to die.

Probably the most dangerous eruption is the *nuée ardente* or "hot cloud." A sudden explosion shoots out a cloud of gas, ash, and lumps of lava, which glide down the slopes like a fast river. There is rarely any warning. Red-hot and almost silent, the cloud kills everything in its path.

Bombs

Gases trapped in the lava may escape in explosions that send blobs of lava into the air. These fall as volcanic bombs. Some are as large as houses!

When volcanic ash settles, it may form a layer many yards deep.

21

Extinct Volcanoes

How do we know when a volcano is truly extinct? Tristan da Cunha, a volcanic island in the South Atlantic, was thought to be extinct for centuries. In 1961, it suddenly erupted and the islanders had to leave for two years. More likely to stay extinct are the volcanoes in the Puys region of France, which last erupted 5,000 years ago. They are worn down by the weather, but their craters and many other surface features can still be seen.

Devil's Tower
This famous piece of rock in Wyoming, USA, was once the lava inside the main vent of a volcano. It has resisted wearing away, and is called a volcanic plug. It featured in Close Encounters of the Third Kind.

Sills and dikes
These hard layers of volcanic rock have resisted wearing away, unlike the surrounding rock, which has been eroded. They stand above the surface like great slabs, sometimes hundreds of miles long.

Crater lake
In an extinct volcano, the original crater may form a caldera (see opposite). Some calderas contain lakes, like Crater Lake in Oregon, USA. It is 6 miles across and 2,000 feet deep.

However, careful studies of the rock layers show that, in the distant past, these volcanoes had been quiet for perhaps 10,000 years. Then they came alive and erupted again. So we can never be sure that these types of volcanoes are truly extinct, even after thousands of years.

Some volcanoes are really extinct, since studies of their rocks show that they have not erupted for millions of years. They are mostly worn away, but parts still remain, making huge features in the landscape. For example, solidified lava in the old vent of a volcano may be harder than the surrounding rocks. They wear away to leave a turret of rock, a volcanic plug, towering above the landscape. There are many such plugs in the Warrumbungles region of Australia.

Caldera

Sometimes a volcanic crater becomes a caldera. This happens when the sides of a volcano collapse inwards, or the magma chamber below empties and the whole mountaintop falls into the hole. Calderas are 3 miles or more across. The largest is Aso, in Japan, which is 14 miles long.

Hot Spots

Most volcanic activity is near the edges of tectonic plates. But some volcanoes appear in the middle of tectonic plates, even in the center of a continent or ocean. These volcanoes seem to be the result of "hot spots" around the Earth.

A hot spot is a plume or bulge of molten rock that constantly rises from below, trying to force its way through any weak point above. If and when this happens, it emerges at the surface as a volcano. In East Africa, hot spots are marked by a cluster of giant volcanoes that stand high above the flat plains. Some are extinct, such as Kilimanjaro in Kenya. Others are active, like Nyiragongo, which has liquid lava bubbling in its crater.

These volcanoes are not on an obvious edge of a tectonic plate. But they are fairly close to the great Rift Valley of East Africa. To the north-east, this

HOT SPOTS ON LAND

Rising from the African plains are huge extinct volcanoes such as Kilimanjaro (19,340 feet tall) and Mount Kenya (17,000 feet). They were formed in the same hot spot way as the Hawaiian Islands. They are in the middle of the tropics, yet high enough to have snow on the summit.

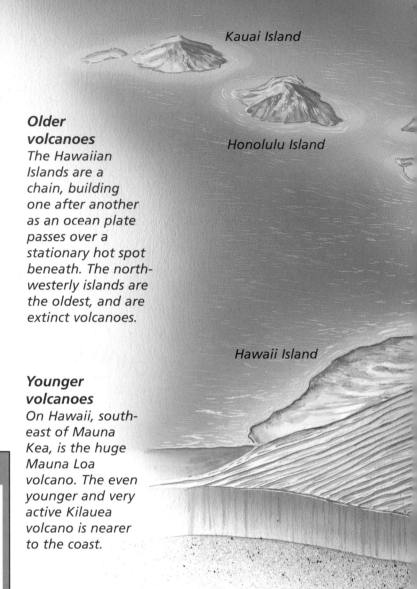

Kauai Island

Honolulu Island

Hawaii Island

Older volcanoes
The Hawaiian Islands are a chain, building one after another as an ocean plate passes over a stationary hot spot beneath. The north-westerly islands are the oldest, and are extinct volcanoes.

Younger volcanoes
On Hawaii, south-east of Mauna Kea, is the huge Mauna Loa volcano. The even younger and very active Kilauea volcano is nearer to the coast.

Baby volcanoes
In the sea east of Hawaii, a new volcanic island has been detected, growing under the sea. This is the site of the same hot spot, deep in the Earth, that built the rest of the Hawaiian chain, as the tectonic plate has moved over it.

Middle aged volcanoes
At the east end of the Hawaii chain is the island of Hawaii itself. To the north-west of the island is the now-extinct volcano of Mauna Kea ("white mountain"), forested and high enough for snow on its summit.

Maui Island

Mauna Kea

Mauna Loa

Magma chamber

Kilauea

Sea-floor sediments

Oceanic crust

valley joins to the Red Sea, which is getting wider as a new mid-oceanic ridge forms along its center. This means the landmasses of Africa and Arabia are slowly separating. In the distant future, Africa may "unzip" down the Rift Valley.

There are hot spots in the oceans, too, along the seabed. They stay in the same place as the tectonic plates slowly move over them, over millions of years. The result is a chain of volcanic islands, with the older islands and their usually extinct volcanoes at one end, and new volcanoes building new islands above the hot spot at the other end. Such a trail stretches across the Indian Ocean. It starts in western India, at the old lava field of the Deccan Plateau (see page 17), passes through Mauritius, and ends at the volcanic island of Réunion, built over the hot spot in the last two million years.

Clouds of Death

The volcano of Vesuvius is in southern Italy, close to the city of Naples. It is the only active volcano on the European mainland. It has periods of quiet, followed by violent eruptions. The last was in 1944, and perhaps another is due. One of Vesuvius' biggest eruptions was in AD 79, the time of Ancient Rome. It was recorded by the Roman writer Pliny the Younger, in a fascinating account of the power and devastation that a volcano can cause. His uncle Pliny the Elder—famous for his enormous series of books titled *Natural Histories*—was one of thousands of Romans who died.

The first indication of trouble was a huge cloud, shaped like a pine tree, from the direction of Vesuvius. A messenger came to the house of Pliny, calling for people to help those across the bay, nearer the mountain. Pliny the Elder commanded a fleet of ships, and set sail to the rescue. As they got closer to the shore on the far side of the bay, hot ashes poured down. Then lumps of pumice rock fell like rain and floated on the water, blocking the way for their ships. They had to change course, and thought of returning, but the wind direction meant that they could not sail back.

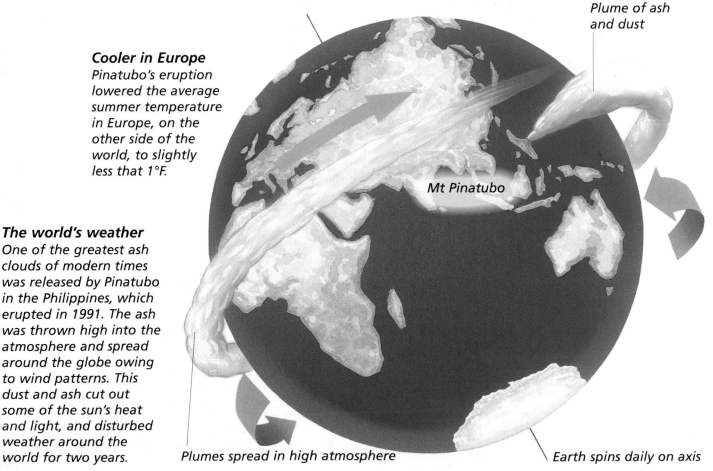

Plume of ash and dust

Cooler in Europe
Pinatubo's eruption lowered the average summer temperature in Europe, on the other side of the world, to slightly less that 1°F.

Mt Pinatubo

The world's weather
One of the greatest ash clouds of modern times was released by Pinatubo in the Philippines, which erupted in 1991. The ash was thrown high into the atmosphere and spread around the globe owing to wind patterns. This dust and ash cut out some of the sun's heat and light, and disturbed weather around the world for two years.

Plumes spread in high atmosphere

Earth spins daily on axis

Pliny and his rescuers went ashore and reassured the inhabitants, spending the night at a villa. Next morning, pumice was falling even harder, like a blizzard of rocky snow. People decided to run to the boats. On the way, Pliny suffocated from the fumes. The day went dark as heavy ash fell thicker. The ground shook, the volcano roared, and earthquakes caused huge waves to crash up and down the coast.

When Vesuvius finally became quiet, two towns had been completely wiped out. One was Pompeii, 6 miles from the volcano. It was covered with a blanket of choking ash and hot pumice up to 25 feet thick. More than 2,000 people died, and the town was abandoned. Yet under the ash, many objects were perfectly preserved—buildings, household utensils, even the shapes of people and animals who did not have time to escape.

In recent years, the deadly blanket over Pompeii has been dug away, to reveal an amazing record of life and death in Ancient Rome. The town of Herculaneum was also buried at the same time, by a lahar, but most of the people had time to flee.

The silent, white blanket
In 1883 the island of Krakatau, South-East Asia, disappeared in an enormous explosive eruption (see page 29). Skies around the world had spectacular sunsets for three years because of the dust thrown into the atmosphere. The dust also decreased the amount of sunlight reaching the surface, so world temperature went down by 1° Fahrenheit. The eruption of Mount Pinatubo in the Philippines in 1991 buried a US base on the island with ash, as shown below.

Volcanoes in History

Through the ages, there have been many enormous volcanic eruptions. Scientists can guess their size by looking at the remains, such as craters, still present today. But only in the past hundred years or so have

Santorini
Date: 1628 BC. Size: 24 cubic miles of material. The eruption cut short the Minoan civilization and affected the whole of the eastern Mediterranean and the Egyptians in North Africa.

Vesuvius
Date: AD 79. Size: 1.5 cubic miles of material. The story of how Vesuvius buried Pompeii is told on the previous page. It was not a vast explosion, but many people lived near by.

Tambora
Date: 1815. Size: 36 cubic miles of material. The eruption on this Indonesian island left an 7-mile crater and 90,000 people dead. This was the biggest eruption by volume.

we been able to measure the real force of a volcanic explosion and monitor the effects with accurate scientific equipment.

In 1628 BC, during the time of Ancient Egypt, the island of Santorini (or Thera), in the Aegean Sea near mainland Greece exploded. The huge eruption sent a column of ash at least 19 miles into the air. The whole center of the island was blown away, leaving just an outer ring. At the time, the Minoans—people with a great civilization—lived on Santorini, nearby Crete, and other islands. So gigantic was the upheaval that the Minoan civilization never recovered its glory and influence.

The effects of the eruption may be recorded in the Bible, in the Exodus stories: "There was a thick darkness in the land of Egypt … pillar of fire and cloud … the waters were divided" (a tsunami?). A layer of ash from this eruption has been identified in Turkey and as far away as the Nile delta.

The biggest volcanic explosion in historic times happened on the island of Krakatau in South-East Asia, in 1883. Two-thirds of the four-mile island were lost in the eruption, which made the loudest noise ever recorded—3,100 miles away it sounded like gunfire. A new volcano, Anak Krakatau ("Krakatau's child") started growing in 1927 in the gap left by Krakatau's disappearance. The 1981 eruption of Mount St. Helens in Washington state was far smaller. Even so, the ash cloud completely circled the world in eleven days.

Krakatau
Date: 1883. Size: 6 cubic miles of material. The biggest explosive force in recent history, this was still only one-sixth the size of Tambora. Over 35,000 were killed by ash, fumes, and waves.

Mount St. Helens
Date: 1980. Size: 0.3 cubic miles of material. Even with plenty of warning, 60 people died as the mountainside blew away. Destruction spread 6 miles; damage was estimated at $3 million.

Mount Pinatubo
Date: 1991. Size: 0.5 cubic miles of material. Massive amounts of ash destroyed hundreds of square miles of farmland and forest, and changed the world's weather for two years.

Pastry Plates

You can imitate the massive movements of tectonic plates at the Earth's surface, using plates made out of pastry. Remember that, with such enormous pressures and forces, even solid rock bends like stiff pastry.

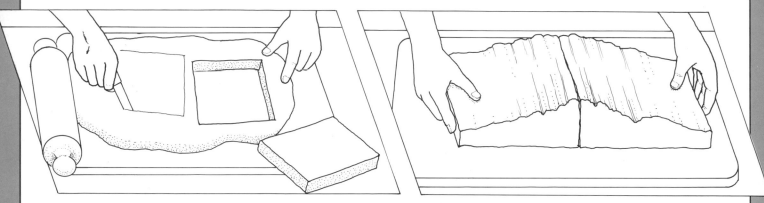

1 *Make an 18-ounce lump of stiff pastry using a cook book recipe. Roll it into a flat slab about 0.5 inches thick. Carefully cut out some blocks, which will be tectonic "pastry plates."*

2 *Put two blocks together so their edges touch. Push them against one another. Do "mountains" form as the pastry plates collide and buckle? In nature, this pushing takes millions of years.*

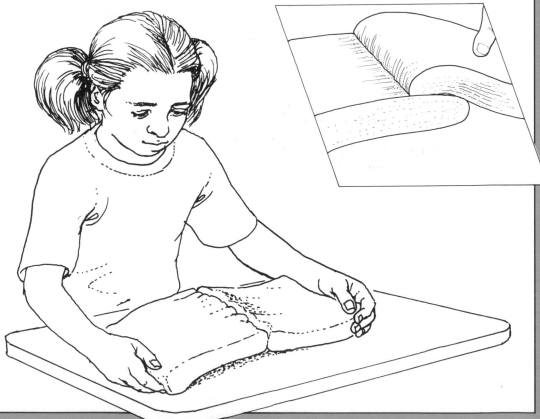

3 *Put two more blocks together so their edges touch. Try to slide them past one another. Do they move smoothly, or do strains, bends, and "earthquakes" develop?*
Put part of one block under the edge of another and push them together. Does this "subduction" work smoothly?

An Erupting Volcano

Make a volcano erupt in your own kitchen! See how the red-hot lava rushes up the chimney of the volcano and flows down its sides. In real life, each eruption would build the volcano's cone higher.

1 Ask if you can borrow a large plate and find a thin bottle about 2.5 inches high. Put the bottle in the middle of the plate. Then build sand or modelling clay around it to form the cone of the volcano. Leave the top of the bottle clear.

2 Cover the kitchen table or counter with newspaper and put the plate on it. Carefully, half-fill the bottle inside the volcano with sodium bicarbonate or Alka Seltzer®. (You can get this from a drug store, food store, or supermarket.)

3 Mix some clear vinegar and some red food coloring together in another bottle or in a measuring jug. Pour the mixture quickly into the mouth of the bottle inside the volcano—and stand well back.

4 Watch as the eruption starts by throwing out foam and then flooding down the sides of the cone.
  If you put the bottle in the cone at a slight angle, what happens?

The giant tectonic plates that make up the Earth's crust move past one another slowly and relentlessly. But they do not always move smoothly. At times they get stuck. Instead of moving, strain builds up in the ground. Sometimes the rocks bend and twist, and cracks or lines of weakness develop, which are called "fault lines." Suddenly, the strain becomes too great. The rocks give way, and the ground on each side of the fault line jumps to a new position. This is an earthquake, one of nature's most powerful events.

During a quake, the land may move only slightly—as little as the width of your finger. Only rarely does it move 50 feet or more. It is also rare to see gaping holes and cracks open up to swallow cars, trains, and buildings. The immense damage to our surroundings is done by the shock waves, or seismic waves, that spread out from the area.

Shock waves
When tension is released in an earthquake, shock or seismic waves travel outwards. Some may be registered on the opposite side of the world. Areas well away from the epicenter may be affected.

HOW THE LAND MOVES

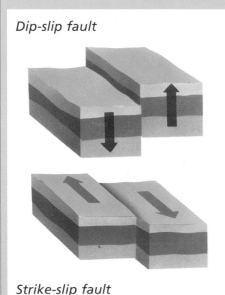

Dip-slip fault

Strike-slip fault

Movement of rocks along a fault may be sideways, or up and down, changing the landscape permanently. In 1923 the huge earthquake in Japan made the seabed sink in some areas by 1,300 feet. The Alaska earthquake of 1964 lifted the land by 26 feet, so that animals and plants that lived along the edge of the sea were left high and dry.

Just as there are extinct volcanoes, there are also extinct fault lines where no movements have taken place for millions of years. The Great Glen of Scotland, now filled by Loch Ness, was an active fault line once, like the San Andreas Fault today.

As explained on page 11, most earthquakes are near the edges of tectonic plates. They can begin as much as 500 miles below the surface, although most are less than 100 miles deep. Often those near the surface cause the most damage. The shaking is much more severe on loose earth, sand, or soft rocks than on hard rock. When these softer substances are vibrated, they act almost like liquids, turning to "quicksand." Buildings, bridges, and other structures topple as though in treacle, or sink into the quicksand. So cities built on these soft rocks are most at risk from earthquake damage.

In California, two of the Earth's tectonic plates—the Pacific and the North American—are moving past one another. The San Andreas Fault, where the slippage occurs, can be seen as a landmark. Many small earthquakes happen along and close to the fault. Occasional large ones cause major damage. This happened in San Francisco in 1906 (see page 40) and again near Los Angeles in 1994.

Fault and fault line
The junction where the two main blocks of rock move past each other is called the fault. It shows on the surface as a fault line.

Epicenter
The epicenter is the place on the surface immediately above the focus. It is what we see as the center of the earthquake. The shock waves appear to spread from here, outward in rings.

Focus
The focus of an earthquake is the point where the slippage and sudden release of energy take place underground. Shock waves of various kinds spread out, gradually weakening.

Studying Earthquakes

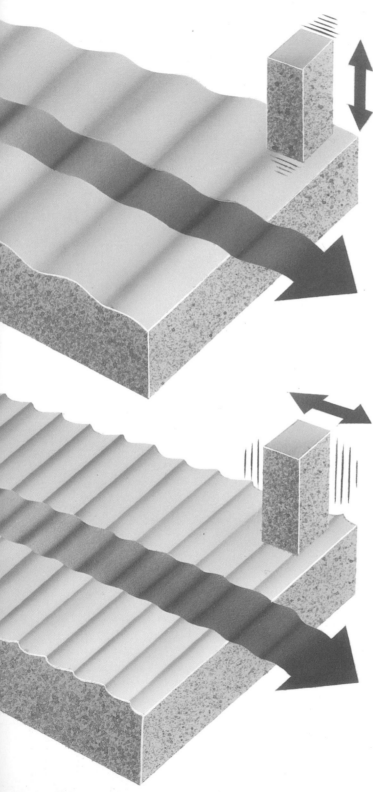

The study of earthquakes is called "seismology," and the people who do it are seismologists. They constantly monitor earthquake activity around the world from their laboratories. They also use automatic equipment and sensors put in remote places, such as high in mountains or on the bottom of the sea, to detect quakes and tremors, and send back information about them over long distances.

The basic device for recording earthquakes and tremors is the seismometer (seismometer, see page 36). A simple version uses a heavily weighted pen suspended by a thin line from a frame. The pen traces a line on a moving strip of paper. In an earthquake, the paper and rest of the device shake,

Secondary (S) waves
Secondary waves, shown above left, are slower than primary waves, below left. They vibrate the rock up and down, like waves on water. People at an earthquake may see the ground thrown into ripples as the S waves pass.

Small earthquake
Less than 4.5

Primary (P) waves
The fastest shock waves from an earthquake are called primary waves. They squeeze or compress the rock as they pass. They can travel right through the Earth and be measured on the other side.

Seismogram
Around the world, all the time, hundreds of seismometers in laboratories are recording the slightest earth tremors as wavy lines. Often, there may be no warning when a "Big One" strikes.

but the pen stays relatively still, hanging on its string. So the pen records a wiggly trace on the paper—a seismogram. Modern seismometers work electronically and can send their information directly to computers, which analyze it and display the results on screen in less than a second.

The to-and-fro shock waves or vibrations of an earthquake may happen in both the horizontal and vertical directions, and seismometers measure these. Some quakes generate waves that run only along the surface. By detecting the arrival times of these different shock waves, at a place far away from the earthquake, it is possible for seismologists to pinpoint the location and strength of the quake. This may be useful for telling the authorities and rescue services, since the earthquake area may have its telephones, TV and radio masts, and other communications damaged.

Various scales are used to measure earthquakes. The Richter scale is shown below. The Mercalli scale measures the intensity of an earthquake by the effects it produces. On this scale, I is hardly noticed; IV is windows rattled and people woken; VIII is general alarm with damage to weaker structures like walls; and XII is total destruction.

Great earthquake
More than 7.5

Major earthquake
6.5 to 7.5

Moderate earthquake
4.5 to 5.5

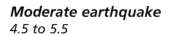

The Richter scale
The Richter scale measures the energy released by an earthquake. Substantial damage is likely at places near a quake that registers 6 or above on this scale. The total destruction seen at XII on the Mercalli scale is likely to happen at about 8.5 on the Richter scale. Every point rise on the Richter scale signals 30 times the energy release of the previous point. So an earthquake at 5 on the Richter scale is 30 times stronger than one that registers 4 on the scale.

Predicting and Preventing

If we could predict earthquakes, it might be possible for many people to avoid death and injury by leaving the area. But, so far, there is no good way of telling when earthquakes will come. Sometimes they announce themselves by small tremors before the main shock, but not always. Some animals seem to behave oddly just before an earthquake, so they may be better than we are at detecting the early signs, but this cannot be done on a reliable scientific basis.

However, we do know where earthquakes are most likely to occur, and, in some areas, roughly how often they happen. But we cannot pinpoint the year, let alone the day, when a major quake will strike. In Japan, a system of seismometers detects earthquakes out at sea that might produce tsunamis.

Chinese detector
This ancient Chinese device has a swinging weight inside a jar. When an earthquake jolts the weight, it pushes a lever that knocks the ball from a dragon's mouth into a frog.

Day in the life of a volcano
This seismic "trace" shows the activity of Stromboli in Sicily during a 24-hour period. The dark areas are earth tremors and mini-earthquakes, caused by the continual bubbling of the volcano.

Warnings can then be flashed on radio and television, giving valuable minutes for people to leave coastal areas.

It seems even less likely that we could prevent earthquakes, given the immense forces involved. Water pumped into wells, in areas where rocks are under strain, can trigger tiny earthquakes. Could this be tried on a much bigger scale, such as on the San Andreas Fault? The idea is that many small earthquakes might prevent one devastating one. It would cost incredible amounts of money and use valuable water. Very few people want to try such an unpredictable and possibly disastrous experiment.

See the Earth Move!

This simple seismometer shows how vibrations and movements, which you might not see, can topple a ball from its precarious perch.

1 Press a lump of modeling clay firmly on to a heavy table's top. Push into it a small candle-holder as used for cake candles, or a golf tee. Make sure this is upright.

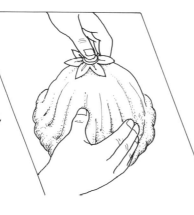

2 Balance a small, light object on top of the candle-holder, such as a table-tennis ball. When an earthquake jolts the area—that is, when you jog the table—the ball will fall!

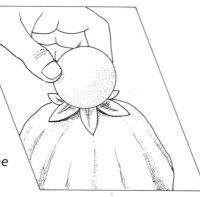

3 You may not have many earthquakes in your area, but you can use your homemade seismometer to test the "shock wave" vibrations from household appliances such as a washing machine or refrigerator, by setting it up on or near them.

Recording Earthquakes

If you have something to suspend a string from, such as a shelf above a table top or similar surface, you could make a seismic recorder. Hang a felt-tip pen from the shelf on a piece of string, weighted with a blob of modeling clay. Adjust it so the pen just rests on a pad of paper on the surface beneath. Jolt the shelf or the table, first with a sharp tap, then with a longer push. What kind of traces do you get on the paper?

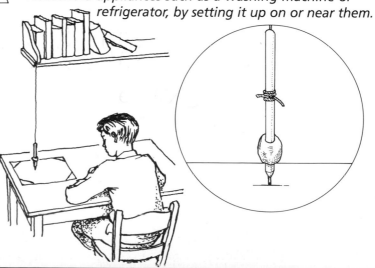

Tsunamis

A tsunami is a giant wave caused by movement of the seabed, owing to a large earthquake or volcanic activity. Sometimes called a "tidal wave," it has nothing to do with tides. It is a massive amount of water set in motion, surging outwards in strong currents from the earthquake or other source. As it nears shallow water at the coast, it builds up like any other wave—but into a giant wall of water, like a breaker many yards high.

The tsunami moves so fast that it can strike virtually without warning, and without time for people to escape. When the volcano Krakatau exploded in 1883 (see page 29), most of the people who died were crushed and drowned by the gigantic tsunamis that swept across nearby islands.

The Pacific Ocean, deep and wide, and rimmed by earthquake and volcano zones, has nine-tenths of all tsunamis. In fact "tsunami" is a Japanese word, and Japan is one of the places most affected. In 1896, a tsunami there killed 27,000 people.

Tsunamis have also struck the Americas and the Hawaiian Islands. After the Hawaiian town of Hilo was devastated in 1946, a tsunami warning system was set up for the Pacific. The wave travels fast, but it still takes nearly a day to cross this ocean. So it is possible to radio ahead and warn areas at risk.

Low but fast
In the open sea, the height of the tsunami is usually less than three feet. So it is hardly noticeable in the general ocean swell. The wave spreads out at speeds up to 500 mph.

Wall of water
When the tsunami approaches a coast, it slows down, but piles up as a wall of water. Funnelled into a narrow coastal inlet, the wave can be more than 65 feet high.

Swept away
The tsunami created by the Krakatau explosion of 1883 was more than 115 feet high. Villages and towns on nearby islands were smashed and swept away. One large steamship was thrown 1.25 miles inland.

Earthquakes in History

In the past century, earthquakes have killed about 15,000 people each year. Some years are worse than others, depending on where the quake happens. For there are big earthquakes every year, but some are high in remote mountains, or under the sea, and hardly anyone is affected. We tend to hear about those quakes which happen in populated areas, where there are many people and buildings.

The number of an earthquake on the Richter or Mercalli scale does not tell how many casualties there will be. Damage and loss of life depends on how populated the nearby areas are, the nature of the ground, and many other factors. If buildings are unstable and not strong, they are more likely to fall down and cause increased injuries and death. If the soils and rocks of the area are soft and loose, they

Devastation through the ages
It is almost certain that, in the next few years, there will be a major earthquake somewhere in the world. The richer industrial nations are able to plan ahead and invest in quake-proof buildings and services. In poor areas, the hazard is part of life—and death.

Gansu, China
This area of China suffered many quakes. The death toll in 1920 was more than 170,000. In 1932, another 70,000 people died in a 7.6 quake.

Date: 1920.
Size: Richter 8.6.

San Francisco, USA
This was the first major earthquake to be measured by modern scientific instruments. About 500 people died as the area's wooden buildings caught fire.

Date: 1906.
Size: Richter 8.3.

Alaska, USA
One of the biggest earthquakes in recent years, this event caused relatively little damage and few deaths—131. This was because it happened in the cold, remote area of Alaska.

Date: 1964.
Size: Richter 8.5.

Tangshan, China
In this crowded city, with a population of 1.6 million people, it is believed that at least 250,000 died as old buildings fell to bits and fires raged in the aftermath.

Date: 1976.
Size: Richter 8.2.

will shake like jelly, and are more likely to cause buildings to collapse. Even the time of day is important. If people are asleep in bed and the quake topples their homes, many more lives will be affected than if people are outside in the open.

Some of the worst earthquake tolls have been in China. In 1556 a huge quake killed an estimated 830,000 people—the worst known loss of life for any earthquake. The numbers were so high because the countryside involved has soft soil which was easily shaken apart, and hills collapsed into valleys. The largest quake in North America may have been in New Madrid, Missouri, in 1812. We cannot be certain, since it was too early for proper scientific measurements. But the shock waves were felt right across America, and the Mississippi River changed its course. The wooden buildings of New Madrid were flattened, but few died in this sparsely populated area. In great contrast, the 1923 Tokyo earthquake killed 143,000 people. Many houses were of traditional wood and paper construction, and they burned readily in the fires that took hold.

Recent years have seen big earthquakes in unexpected places. In 1993 a quake hit the Deccan Plateau in India (see page 17). Most of the stone-and-mud buildings collapsed, killing 10,000 people who were mostly indoors at night. Yet there was no evidence of previous earthquake-type activity for millions of years. A nearby river had been dammed. Perhaps the weight of the water triggered the quake.

Mexico City, Mexico
The biggest city on Earth was hit and 7,200 people lost their lives. There was massive damage and a worldwide rescue effort. The poor shanty towns were soon rebuilt.

Date: 1985.
Size: Richter 8.1.

California, USA
The worst quake in the area for 23 years was not on the main San Andreas Fault but at a minor fault at nearby Northridge. About 60 people died.

Date: 1994.
Size: Richter 6.6.

Kobe, Japan
The focus was shallow, 6 miles underground and 15 miles from Kobe. The port's many traditional wooden houses with heavy tile roofs fell in, crushing sleeping families.

Date: 1995.
Size: Richter 7.2.

Defences Against Quakes

It is not likely that the millions of people in places at risk of quakes, such as Los Angeles or Tokyo, will move away from their cities. However, the possible damage can be reduced by suitably designed buildings, roadways, and railways. These should be flexible and "give," swaying with the tremors, rather than being too rigid and cracking apart. The thin walls and concrete floor slabs used in so many modern tall buildings are very likely to collapse.

It is also important to construct new buildings in the safest areas of the city, where the ground and bedrock are hard and firm. In many Japanese cities, gas supplies automatically cut off if there is an earthquake, so escaping gas does not fuel fires.

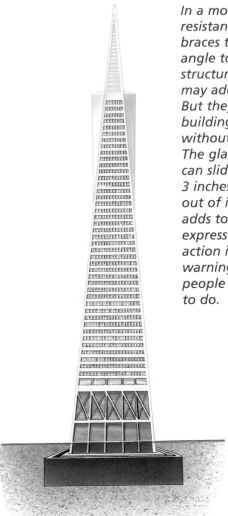

Able to twist
In a modern quake-resistant design, steel braces that run at an angle to the main structure of a skyscraper may add weight and cost. But they allow the building to twist and flex without coming apart. The glass in the windows can slide and move up to 3 inches without falling out of its frame, which adds to safety. Special express lifts come into action if there is a quake warning, and all the people inside know what to do.

Based on rubber
Modern buildings in earthquake-prone regions are built to new guidelines. They may have rubber shock absorbers in their foundations. Hanging the floors and walls from a steel frame, rather than rigid joints, also helps.

Also, if main roads are built through relatively open areas and do not get torn up or blocked by fallen buildings, then emergency vehicles can arrive more effectively. All these measures can help.

In 1987, a shock of 6.6 on the Richter scale hit Tokyo, but little damage was done to the specially designed buildings. In this city of 10 million people, only two lost their lives. This contrasts with the chaos and destruction in the mainly old city of Kobe, when the earthquake struck in 1995.

Tsunamis in Your Bath!

You could create a tsunami ("huge wave") in your bath. Hold your hands as though about to clap underwater, on the bath's bottom. Bring them together strongly, like two tectonic plates moving together. See the tsunami as the water surges and waves swell up and outwards! (However, avoid flooding the bathroom floor!)

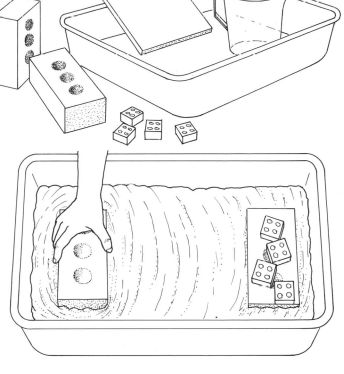

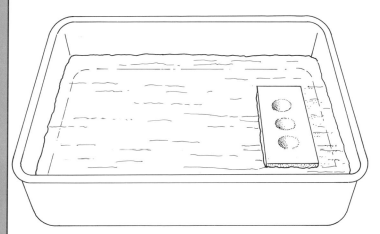

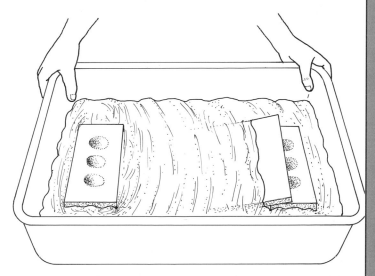

1 *In a safe place where water spills do not matter, fill a large bowl or baby bath with water. Place a house brick at one end. Adjust the water so the brick's top is just above the surface. This is a low-lying tropical island in the earthquake zone.*

2 *Put some small building blocks or similar on the brick, to represent houses on the island. Put another brick or stone at the other end of the bowl.*

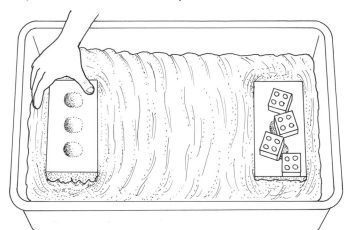

3 *Gently lift this second brick slightly, then release it. This is the massive energy release of an earthquake. A mini-tsunami sweeps across the sea to the island. What effect does it have?*

4 *Take away the blocks and place a large tile on the brick, sloping into the water. This is a beach. Make some more tsunamis. How do the waves run up the slope? Does its steepness make any difference?*

Helpful Volcanoes

Volcanoes can spit death and spurt destruction across the world. Yet they have also helped humankind and shaped our history in various ways, as shown in the following pages. During the Age of Exploration (1415–1778), European-based sailors braved the perils of the open ocean to find new lands and show that the world was indeed a globe. Many died tragically, lost in the vastness of the seas. More would have disappeared, if it had not been for mid-ocean islands—volcanic in origin—where they could stop and gather supplies of food and water.

People had already spread around the world centuries before, by island-hopping in stages. Across the Pacific Ocean, in particular, they migrated from one volcanic island group to the next, establishing settlements and distinctive cultures, then moving on to colonize more islands.

Philippines
With more than 7,000 volcanic islands, this country was populated by waves of immigrants, mainly from Indonesia. Today it has a rich mosaic of cultures based on Malay, with many Eastern and Western influences.

Antilles Islands

Galápagos Islands

Fiji

Maoris
The Maori people of New Zealand probably arrived there in the 12th century, as canoe travellers from the islands of Polynesia.

Easter Island
Tiny and remote, this volcanic island is famous for its stone statues of giant heads. They were carved by the settlers who came from South America or Polynesia.

Canary Islands

A group of volcanic islands off North Africa, the Canaries have been Spanish since 1479. Christopher Columbus used them as supply stops on his voyages to the New World of the Americas.

Madeira

Azores

From the 1930s, mid-ocean islands formed by volcanoes were important in establishing long-haul air travel. They were stop-over and refuelling places for long journeys, when planes could not fly as far as they do today. The ports and airports of volcano-formed islands, especially in the Pacific, have been a vital part of strategic planning in wartime. In 1942, the Battle of Midway, fought on a tiny volcanic coral island in the central Pacific, was a turning point in World War Two. So volcanic islands have had great effects on the course of history, from human migrations in prehistoric times, to the modern era of diving holidays on coral reefs (see page 66).

Across the Pacific

Polynesians used canoes similar to these, to island-hop on their voyages of exploration.

Ascension

This small volcanic island just south of the Equator had an important air base during World War Two.

The Falkland Islands and South Georgia

South Georgia was a base for the huge whaling ships that slaughtered thousands of great whales, from about 1910 to 1950. They helped the growth of trade, although they also contributed to the danger of extinction that whales now face.

Mauritius

This volcanic island was colonized many times by different countries, including France, Britain, India, and China. This was because of its important position on the sailing trade routes between Europe, Africa, and the Middle and Far East.

Constant Hot Water

As you dig deeper in the Earth, so you get nearer the hot, molten rock beneath, and the temperature rises. Deep in a mine, it can be very hot. It is sometimes possible to extract the heat from deep rocks and use it for industry—to make hot water, and to provide heating for buildings.

Under Paris, the spongy, waterlogged rocks about 6,500 feet down contain plenty of hot water. It is worth drilling down to tap this energy source. The water comes to the surface at between 140° and 212° Fahrenheit, and is used to provide heating and hot water for several large buildings. Unfortunately, the hot water is not replaced as fast as it is being used, so the scheme is gradually running down.

Near areas of volcanic activity, this heating effect is even more marked. Even when volcanic eruptions in an area die out, there may still be vast, hot lumps of rock underground that can warm the water trickling down through them.

Geysers
In some areas, water trickles down into the rocks and gets so hot that it boils. The pressure carries a column of water up a crack and shoots it into the air. This natural fountain is a geyser. Some geysers erupt with great regularity. Since records began, Old Faithful in Yellowstone Park has erupted about every hour, shooting water up to 200 feet.

As geysers die
Some geysers gradually lose their power and stop erupting as the volcanic heat dies down. This happened to Iceland's Great Geysir, which gave its name to all other geysers. Waimangu Geyser in New Zealand has also faded since about 1905. But it still holds the world record for height at 1,640 feet.

BOILING MUD POOLS

Inside a geyser

Rain water seeps through cracks in the rocks, and collects in a large cave-like chamber. The heat from below makes it boil and turn to steam. This increases the pressure as bubbles of steam build up. Finally the pressure is enough to shoot the water and steam upwards and out, high into the air.

In the same way that superheated water squirts from a geyser, underground heat can also make water, minerals, and rock particles mix and boil, in a bubbling mud pool. This can be very dangerous when fully active. The mud is so hot that it burns skin at once, and a spurt of pressure can splatter boiling-hot mud for many feet around.

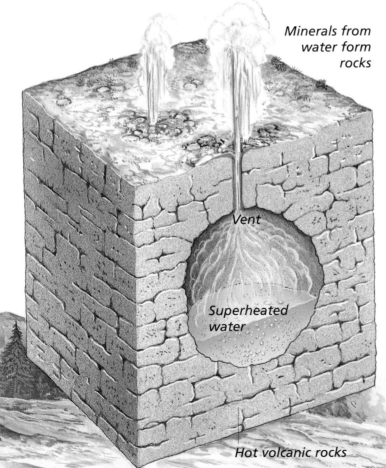

Fountain of water and steam

Minerals from water form rocks

Vent

Superheated water

Hot volcanic rocks

Sometimes the water emerges at the surface as a hot spring. This water may be pure and clear, but usually has many minerals dissolved in it, which have come from the rocks. As the water cools around the edges of the pool or spring, the minerals form crystals and grains. These build up into beautiful rock layers shaped like waves, basins and terraces. Japan, New Zealand, Iceland, and Yellowstone Park in the Rocky Mountains have many such mineral-rich hot springs.

The water in hot springs can be nearly boiling yet there are some living things which can survive in it. The springs may be colored in reds, greens, and blues by microscopic bacteria and simple, plant-like algae that grow in clumps and mats. Away from the fiercest heat, insects and other animals live in the water. In hot springs by Lake Magadi, Kenya, there are dwarf tilapia fish grazing on the algae, in water at 104° Fahrenheit—as hot as a bathtub. Some hot springs are so full of particles of rock, carried up by the water, that they are little more than liquid mud which plops and boils.

Hot volcanic springs feed several of the lakes in East Africa's Rift Valley. In some, the water contains so much soda mineral that hardly anything can live, except a few types of algae. Yet lesser flamingos wade into the lakes and eat this food source.

Volcanoes and Farming

On a volcano's slopes
The soils formed from lava and ash are rich in nutrients, and hold water well. Grape vines are planted on the higher slopes, with fruit bushes and trees such as oranges and lemons on the lower slopes. But the volcano far above may be an ever-present threat.

Although volcanoes can cause enormous destruction of crops, livestock, and farmland, they can also benefit agriculture. Hot volcanic ash and lava burns and kills. But once the ash and rock particles have cooled and the volcanic activity has stopped, then the wind, rain, sun, and forces of erosion get to work on them. Over many years, the ash and lava can turn into nutrient-rich soils. The many minerals in volcanic rock improve the soil's richness, and various types of plants thrive in it. Around the world, different types of volcanic soils, old and new, are used for farming.

In the Canary Islands, the volcanic soil is very fertile and supports intense agriculture. Some of the world's best coffee grows on the slopes of Central American volcanoes. In Indonesia, much of the best growing land is near volcanoes. On the slopes of Mount Etna in Italy, fruit trees and vines thrive.

This rich agricultural land is the reason why many people settle in clusters around active volcanoes, rather than avoiding them. The people know there is a risk, but they believe that it is worth taking, for the richness of the land and soils. A small eruption may even be welcomed if it provides a light fall of nourishing ash, which the rain soon waters into the ground. Even where volcanoes are long extinct, agriculture may follow a pattern that reveals the ash falls of long ago, as has been found around some Australian hills.

Volcanoes and Industry

Rocks and minerals
Pumice stone (see page 20)
is one of many useful
volcanic substances. It is
used as an abrasive, either
in washing or industrially.
It also makes large, light
blocks for building.

In volcanic areas, useful heat may be at or near the
surface of the ground. So it is worthwhile installing
pipes and equipment to obtain it, especially if the
heat is replaced as fast as it can be carried away and
used. This is called "geothermal energy," and it may
be obtained in various ways.

In some places geysers and hot springs bubble at
the surface. It may be possible to pipe this hot
water and use it to warm buildings and water
supplies, and provide heat for industrial processes
and leisure activities. In Iceland, some lakes are
warm enough for bathing, even in winter. Here
and in Japan, hot water from volcanic sources is
diverted to swimming pools.

Towns near this natural hot water can use it for
many purposes. In New Zealand, the town of
Rotorua makes good use of "free" hot water for

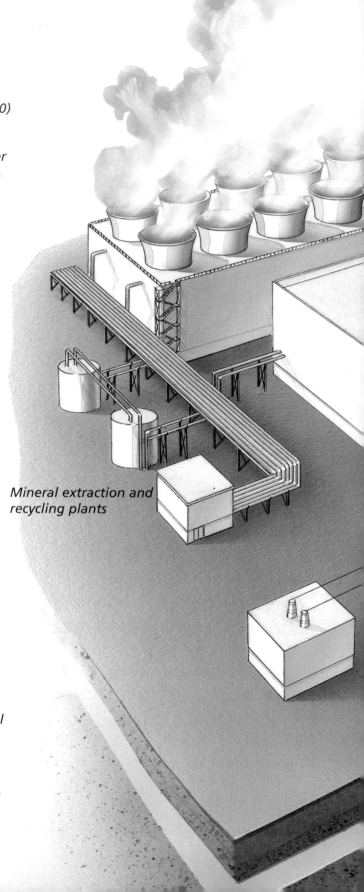

Mineral extraction and
recycling plants

Metals and gems
Gold, copper, and silver
may be found in old
volcanoes. They have
been purified by natural
volcanic activity. At
Kimberley, South Africa,
the depths of an old
volcano contain the
richest concentration of
diamonds in the world.

50

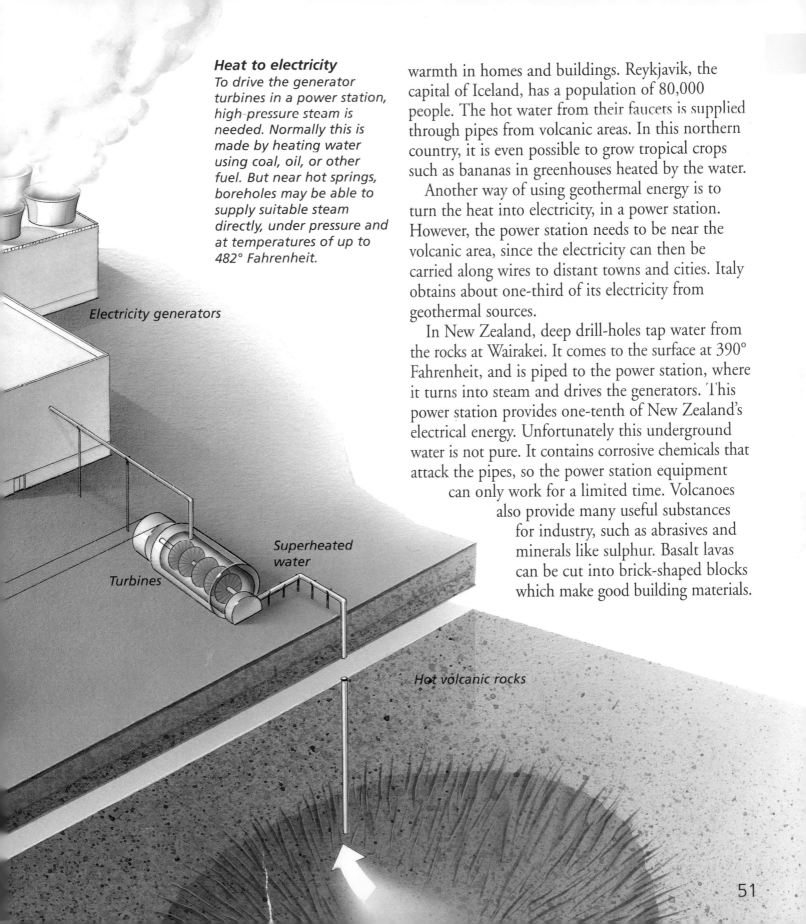

Heat to electricity

To drive the generator turbines in a power station, high-pressure steam is needed. Normally this is made by heating water using coal, oil, or other fuel. But near hot springs, boreholes may be able to supply suitable steam directly, under pressure and at temperatures of up to 482° Fahrenheit.

Electricity generators

Turbines

Superheated water

Hot volcanic rocks

warmth in homes and buildings. Reykjavik, the capital of Iceland, has a population of 80,000 people. The hot water from their faucets is supplied through pipes from volcanic areas. In this northern country, it is even possible to grow tropical crops such as bananas in greenhouses heated by the water.

Another way of using geothermal energy is to turn the heat into electricity, in a power station. However, the power station needs to be near the volcanic area, since the electricity can then be carried along wires to distant towns and cities. Italy obtains about one-third of its electricity from geothermal sources.

In New Zealand, deep drill-holes tap water from the rocks at Wairakei. It comes to the surface at 390° Fahrenheit, and is piped to the power station, where it turns into steam and drives the generators. This power station provides one-tenth of New Zealand's electrical energy. Unfortunately this underground water is not pure. It contains corrosive chemicals that attack the pipes, so the power station equipment can only work for a limited time. Volcanoes also provide many useful substances for industry, such as abrasives and minerals like sulphur. Basalt lavas can be cut into brick-shaped blocks which make good building materials.

Mimic an Earthquake

You might not be able to see the vibrations of an earthquake pass through solid rock. But you can see them as jumping grains of sand, salt, or sugar.

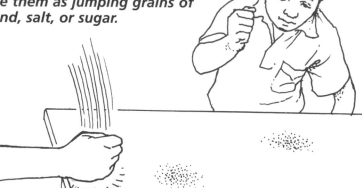

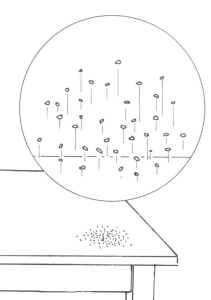

1 On a long and fairly lightweight table, which can bend slightly, scatter some grains of sand. Bang the edge of the table with your hand. This is the focus of the earthquake.

2 See how the vibrations or shock waves travel through the table, by the way the sand grains move and jump. Bang the table at different places. Are the shock waves as strong all the way along? Are there some places where they are weaker, perhaps because the "rock layers" of the table are stiffer, such as in the corners?

Shaking the Ground

3 Slide your hand holding the comb deep into the

Earthquakes are so big that it's hard to see what really happens. This experiment shows you how the ground is shaken about when two giant earth plates try to jerk past each other, deep underground. You will need to borrow an old plastic washing-up bowl.

1 Fill the plastic washing-up bowl to the top with fine sand. (Ordinary soil or earth is not suitable.)

2 Next find an old plastic comb. It should have flexible teeth, so that you can flick them down with your thumb.

bowl and smooth the sand over. Flick the comb's teeth hard with your thumb. Watch the vibrations show as patterns in the sand.

Volcanoes and Wildlife

Volcanoes, earthquakes, and the landscapes they create have an enormous influence on wildlife. Through the ages, plants, and animals change or evolve. If they are in a small and limited area, such as on a volcanic island in an ocean, or in a valley bordered by earthquake fault lines, then evolution tends to happen more quickly. It produces new and distinctive species of plants and animals, each adapted to its individual and unique surroundings.

Volcanic islands like the Hawaiian and Galápagos groups are "natural laboratories of evolution." Biologists can trace how a few living things arrived at the newly formed islands, and then multiplied, spread and evolved to fit the unique surroundings.

Occasionally volcanoes have a more direct use for animals. The maleo bird of Sulawesi, Indonesia, uses beaches of black volcanic sand as a nest site. The sun warms the black sand and the bird does not need to sit on its eggs—it simply buries them.

MOUNTAIN EVOLUTION

As volcanoes build mountains in the landscape, plants and animals spread up their slopes. Separated from their neighbors on other mountains, these living things evolve in their own distinct way, into new varieties or species. The axolotl is a salamander (a type of amphibian) which is found only in the Lake Xochimilco region, among the high volcanic mountains of Mexico. Many other volcanic peaks and ranges have their own kinds of flowers, insects, lizards, rabbits, mice, and even flying creatures such as butterflies and birds.

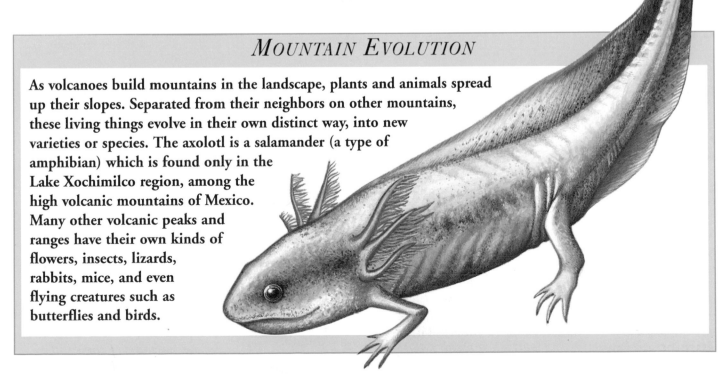

On the Deep Seabed

Where there is volcanic activity on the sea floor, as along mid-oceanic ridges, there can be underwater hot springs. In 1963 these were first noticed in the new ridge on the bottom of the Red Sea. Like hot springs on land, the undersea spring squirts out hot, mineral-rich water through holes or cracks, which are called deep-sea hydrothermal vents.

In 1977 a deep-sea research vessel studied the mid-oceanic ridge system near the Galápagos Islands. On the seabed 8,200 feet below the surface, it found places where vents on the ocean floor blasted out water superheated to 662° Fahrenheit.

The biggest surprise for the expedition was to find whole communities of living things around these hydrothermal vents, in the black depths of the sea. Their basic food is the energy-rich minerals in the vent water, which is used by microbes such as bacteria. These are eaten in turn by larger animals— some of the strangest creatures in the world.

Black smokers
As hot water from a vent mixes with the surrounding sea water at 39° Fahrenheit and cools, its dissolved salts and sulfide minerals form crystals and tiny particles. These make a dense, dark cloud, so the vents are called "black smokers."

Shellfish
Deep-sea mussels as big as your hand, and clams the size of dinner plates, feed by filtering the bacteria from the water. Small, white, eyeless crabs scavenge around the clusters of worms and shellfish.

Submersibles
Only a few vessels can dive to great depths. The US deep-sea submersible Alvin first discovered and studied hydrothermal vents.

Fish
The rising hot water makes currents that swirl around bits and pieces of debris, such as rotting flesh from creatures who died far above. These edible bits feed deep-sea fish, who also benefit from the warmth of the nearby vent as they scavenge on the seabed.

Worms
Massive tube-worms, up to 12 feet long and as thick as your wrist, live in colonies around the vents. They feed on the plentiful microscopic bacteria. The worms have no mouths. They absorb the bacteria through the thin skin of their tentacles.

The Arrival of Life

New land
Near Iceland, the new island of Surtsey first appeared as steam in the empty sea. Lava at 1,830° Fahrenheit boiled sea water and fumes rose up 5 miles. Once above the surface, the eruption quietened, but lava continued to pour out for some months.

When the volcanic island of Krakatau blew up in 1883, the small part that remained was covered in searing-hot ash and pumice up to 130 feet thick. Every living thing on the island must have died. But the island, now called Rakata, did not remain lifeless for long. A few months after the explosion, a French expedition landed to make scientific surveys. Wind, sun, and rain were breaking up the rock and ash into soil. There was a sign of new life—a tiny spider spinning a web. One year later, a few grass shoots appeared. Three years after the eruption, fifteen kinds of shrubs and grasses were growing. A year later, there were forty-nine kinds.

Animals moved in, too. An early arrival was a python, perhaps carried out to sea on a raft of branches. Rats arrived, and various kinds of lizards, probably on drifting tree trunks and branches. Some may have floated or swum by themselves. The common Asiatic monitor lizard swims well and sometimes takes to sea—it reached Rakata. Birds, bats and butterflies flew in. Small insects, spiders, and the seeds and spores of plants and fungi get blown long distances, and they also arrived.

By 1920 the island's main vegetation was grassland, with some patches of forest. Today, Rakata is once again clothed in tropical forest.

Groundsel and similar "parachute" seeds float far over the ocean.

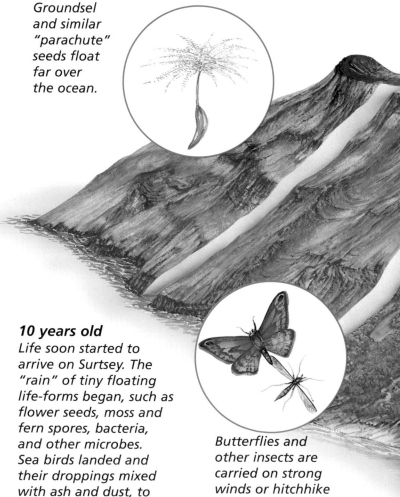

10 years old
Life soon started to arrive on Surtsey. The "rain" of tiny floating life-forms began, such as flower seeds, moss and fern spores, bacteria, and other microbes. Sea birds landed and their droppings mixed with ash and dust, to begin soil formation.

Butterflies and other insects are carried on strong winds or hitchhike on birds.

There are now thirty kinds of birds, about average for an island this size. There are nine species of bats, the same number of reptiles, and over 600 kinds of insects, worms, and similar small creatures.

Near Rakata, in place of the original Krakatau, a new volcanic island has appeared, Anak Krakatau. Experiments showed that a constant "rain" of spiders and insects falls from the air. Most perish, but from the few survivors, new life begins. Even the bodies of those that die help to enrich the new soil.

Another natural laboratory was provided by the eruption of a volcano off the southern coast of Iceland in 1963–4. It created a new island, Surtsey, about 6,500 feet across and 568 feet high. Some of the first seeds to arrive were groundsels, whose fluffy parachutes carried them from Iceland itself. In 1965, a survey found one type of large plant, six species of flies and two types of moths. By 1967 there were four kinds of land plants, and seaweeds and shellfish along the shores. Birds—fulmars and guillemots—began nesting in 1970. Silver-Y moths have also been found on Surtsey. They do not live in Iceland, so they may have come all the way from Britain. The undersea volcano has created a whole new world for nature.

Guillemots and other sea birds now live on Surtsey.

20 years old
Many parts of Surtsey, once harsh dark lava, are now tinged with green. Every year, on average, one new kind of plant is established. Many grow from seeds in bird droppings. Surtsey's position on a bird migration route has probably helped to speed its colonization.

Snow buntings fly in from Scotland.

The Hawaiian Islands

Beaks and food
The Hawaiian honeycreepers have developed different-shaped beaks, to eat the many kinds of food on the different islands. Their colors have also evolved over thousands of years.

Akohekohe
This honeycreeper probes into flowers for nectar with its long, slim beak.

Akiola
The long, tweezer-like beak picks small insects from cracks in tree bark.

Maui parrotbill
The strong beak tears up tree bark, to get at insect grubs.

Remote volcanic islands provide perfect places to study how living things change and evolve to fit their surroundings. One of the best examples is the Hawaiian Islands. They are very remote, about 1,865 miles from the nearest continent. Even so, they were colonized by plants and animals soon after they formed, when a hot spot caused a chain of seabed volcanoes (see page 24). The main islands range in age from about 5.6 million years for Kauai in the north-west, to about 400,000 years for Hawaii itself in the south-east.

When plants and animals arrive in an empty land, strange things can happen. Evolution runs riot because, in the early years, there is plenty of space to live and grow, yet few predators. Plants which are small elsewhere can become huge. On Hawaii, plants of the dandelion family have become tree-sized. The familiar insects called lacewings, with their beautiful and delicately traced wings, have become completely wingless. At some time, a single species of tiny fruit fly

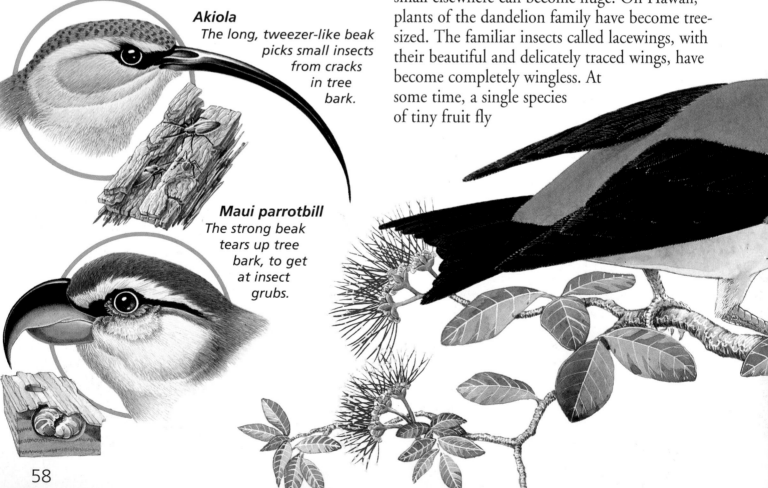

(*Drosophila*) seems to have made its way to Hawaii, perhaps carried on strong winds. From this, 500 new and different species have descended, which are found nowhere else in the world. Some are giants compared to the "normal" gnat-sized fruit flies.

Biologists estimate that perhaps 500 species of insects arrived in Hawaii from elsewhere. All of the 10,000 insect species now living there have evolved from them. They include some real oddities. Dragonfly larvae (nymphs) are normally aquatic, living in ponds and hunting worms and tadpoles. But in Hawaii, one species has left the water to hunt on the forest floor. There are also many colorful and unique birds, especially the honeycreepers shown here. However, all around the world, island wildlife is at risk as people bring cats, dogs, rats, and other animals to destroy the balance of nature created by volcanic activity.

Kona grosbeak
This bird's powerful beak can crush and chop up hard seeds and nuts.

Ou
The strong parrot-like beak cuts and crushes fruits and soft seeds.

Akiapolauu
The lower part of the beak chisels away bark, and the upper part tweaks out small grubs.

The original honeycreeper?
The Hawaiian honeycreepers are probably descended from one species of canary-like finch that arrived on the islands thousands of years ago. When Captain Cook came to Hawaii in 1778, 28 of the 70 or so native bird species were honeycreepers. Sadly, at least eight are probably now extinct.

ENDANGERED SNAILS

The Hawaiian Islands are home to a group of 189 species of tree snails, called partulas. They are thought to have evolved from a single ancestor species. Some live in only one or two valleys, isolated by high mountain ridges. Tragically, other snails which have been brought by people now endanger many partulas. The partula snails provide a fantastic example of evolution in action—and also of the dangers of extinction on small islands.

Standing up to Earthquakes

You can investigate designs for earthquake-proof buildings, using only Scotch® tape and drinking straws! The straws represent the huge steel girders which make up the framework or "skeleton" of a large, tall building such as a skyscraper. You tape them together in different patterns and designs, then tape the whole framework to a tray, in the same way that buildings have foundations in the ground. Shaking the tray mimics an earthquake, and shows if the building frame is strong or if it twists, buckles, and collapses.

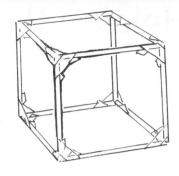

1 Investigate the normal girder design for skyscrapers by making box-shaped cubes with straws. Make a two-story building, tape it to the tray, and shake hard. Does it survive the tremors?

2 How many stories could be built like this, and still resist the shaking of an earthquake? Add one or two floors, and test the design again by shaking the tray.

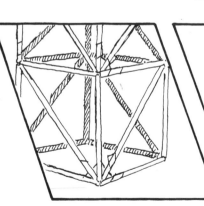

3 Keep adding extra stories to make the skyscraper higher. Eventually, the girder framework is too tall. When the quake hits, it bends and falls, partly under its own weight.

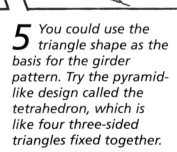

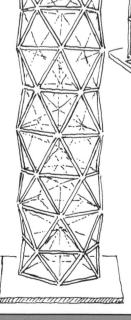

4 Try steps 1 to 3 again, but strengthen the frames with diagonal crosspieces. These form triangles instead of squares. The triangle is a much stronger structural shape, and it should help to keep the building upright.

5 You could use the triangle shape as the basis for the girder pattern. Try the pyramid-like design called the tetrahedron, which is like four three-sided triangles fixed together.

6 Join many tetrahedrons to build up a skyscraper. Shake it regularly to see how high it can go, before it collapses. Is it stronger than a structure of the same height made from cubes? Would triangular rooms be useful?

Helping the Fossil-Hunters

Fossils are the remains of animals and plants that lived long ago, preserved in the rocks and turned to stone. The fossils are usually hard parts such as bones, teeth, claws, horns, shells, bark, and seeds that do not rot away quickly after death. They settle onto the ground, usually under water, in sediments such as sand, clay, mud, or silt. More sediments settle on top and bury them. The buried sediments and the bits and pieces they contain are squashed and hardened into layers of rock, known as strata. Millions of years later, earth movements lift the strata—and an earthquake cracks them open to reveal the fossils!

1 *Make several large, flat, sheet-like pieces from modelling clay or a similar substance. These are the rock layers, or strata. It is best if they are different colors.*

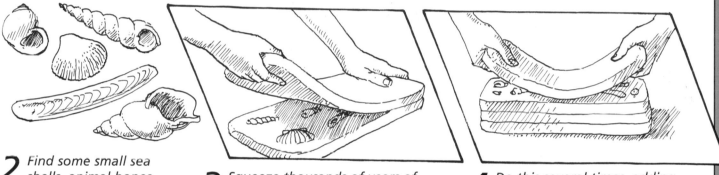

2 *Find some small sea shells, animal bones and similar items to be the "fossils." Or make your own fossils, such as dinosaur teeth and bones, from papier mâché.*

3 *Squeeze thousands of years of rock formation into a minute! Place a few "fossils" on a layer of "rock." Add another rock layer on top, like sediments settling onto the seabed.*

4 *Do this several times, adding more fossils and then another rock layer or stratum. In real life, the strata could be hundreds of feet thick and millions of years old.*

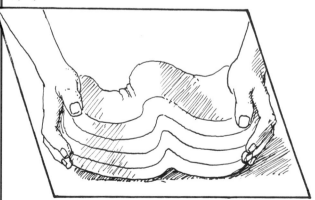

5 *When you have finished, bend and buckle the whole thick, multi-layered sandwich. This represents the huge, slow movements of the Earth's crust.*

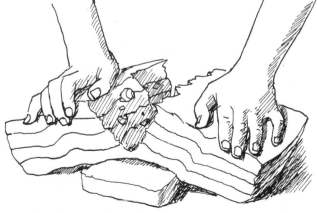

6 *Now for the earthquake. Crack or slice through the layers, or pull them apart. With luck, you can see the different rock strata, and perhaps some fossils, too. Even expert fossil-hunters need plenty of luck to find the best specimens.*

The Galápagos Islands

The Galápagos Islands lie in the Pacific Ocean, nearly 620 miles west of South America. They were formed by volcanic eruptions on the seabed less than one million years ago. Relatively few land creatures have managed to make the hazardous journey across the sea to them.

There is a great amount of chance in which kinds of plants and animals reach a volcanic island in the middle of the ocean. There are many influences, such as the distance to the nearest mainland, wind patterns and water currents.

Although the Galápagos are on the Equator, the Peru Ocean Current makes the climate cool and dry, so conditions for life are not as kind as on the Hawaiian Islands. However, once plants and animals had reached the Galápagos, they changed and evolved as they adapted to the different conditions on the thirteen main islands and the many smaller ones. This has all happened in tens of thousands of years. In the scale of the Earth's whole history, it is just the twinkling of an eye.

Woodpecker finch
This species is skilled at using cactus spines to prise out small animals.

Isabela Island

Fernandina Island

Large ground finch
The large beak of this bird crushes hard nuts and seeds.

Sea lizards
It seems that iguana lizards reached the Galápagos at some time, and evolved into two different species. One is the marine iguana, the only lizard that swims well in the sea and feeds there. It is found nowhere else in the world.

Marchena Island

Darwin's finches

Small finches from South America arrived in the Galápagos, perhaps blown on a strong wind. Their descendants now make up thirteen different species of "Darwin's finches" on the islands. They are rather similar in shape and dull in color, but their beaks are adapted in various ways to eat different foods.

Large tree finch

This species pecks at spiders, beetles, and grubs in the tree bark.

San Salvador Island

Santa Cruz Island

The Galápagos are especially important because an English naturalist visited them in 1835. His name was Charles Darwin. He noted how each island seemed to have its own types of animals, such as birds, insects, tortoises, and other creatures—yet they were all quite similar to the equivalent species on other islands in the group. There was also a general similarity of the wildlife to the plants and animals he had seen earlier, in western South America. From these observations, Darwin developed the idea of evolution by natural selection, one of the main theories of modern science.

Island animals have a strange tendency to lose their wings and become flightless. Perhaps in the early days, there were few predators for flying animals, so they had little need of wings. Some Galápagos grasshoppers have tiny wings, and the Galápagos cormorant is completely flightless.

Cactus ground finch

The small beak is designed for probing into the flowers of the prickly-pear cactus.

San Cristóbal Island

Galápagos giant tortoises

Floating across the sea to the Galápagos Islands from South America came a tortoise, perhaps a female ready to lay eggs. Her descendants populated other islands and changed to become larger than their mainland ancestors, and different from each other.

Warbler finch

This small bird's slim beak snaps up tiny insects, sometimes in mid air.

Santa Maria Island

63

Crater Wildlife Parks

Africa in miniature

Smaller than Ngorongoro, but also good for wildlife, is Ngurdoto Crater near Arusha. It is only 1.5 miles across, but has a well-watered floor and wooded rim. People are not allowed on to the crater floor, but they can view the abundant wildlife from the rim. It is like a gigantic, natural wild park.

The remains of old volcanoes provide craters and calderas which can be havens for wildlife. The vast caldera of Ngorongoro lies in Tanzania, Africa. It is 12 miles long, 10 miles wide, 116 square miles in area, and some 2,130 feet below the surrounding rim. The Ngorongoro contains lakes, woodlands, and grasslands, and is a nature reserve.

The shape of the land means that wardens patrolling the volcano's old rim can see far across the crater, to watch for poachers and other dangers.

Zebra

Giraffe

Lion cubs

Lions feed on a kill.

Naturalists can monitor the movements of lions, wildebeest, zebra, and other animals.

Volcanic mountains such as Kilimanjaro and Mt Kenya (see page 24) provide the opposite. They are islands of cool habitats rising from the sea of the hot African grasslands. A climber would ascend from the dry plains, through broad-leaved forests and then conifer forests, before reaching moorland, then grassy meadows, and finally the snow and ice on the summit. Like other "islands," these mountains enrich the landscape and are home to their own varieties and species of living things.

Ecology in action
Volcanic craters and calderas provide excellent sites for surveying wildlife, counting the populations of various plants and animals, and studying how they are affected by drought, fire, and similar events.

Wildebeest (gnu)

Ostriches

Impala

Antelope

Hyenas and vultures scavenge a carcass.

Coral Reefs and Atolls

Corals are tiny animals that look like miniature sea anemones and live in large colonies. Some kinds make stony, cup-shaped skeletons around their bodies, for support and protection. Over many years, millions of these stony skeletons can build up into enormous underwater structures called reefs.

Reef-building corals live in warm seas, where the average temperature is more than 68° Fahrenheit. The corals are in partnership with tiny plants— algae—living inside their bodies. The algae need light to grow, so coral reefs form only where the water is clear and bright, less than about 100 feet in depth. Some coral reefs develop at the edge of the land, along tropical shores. They are fringing reefs. Other reefs grow in ring shapes around islands and are known as barrier reefs. Still others form a circle or oval called an atoll, with no land in the middle. The tops of the reef may show as a broken ring of small islands. How does all this happen? As shown here, the answer is: volcanoes!

Stage 1
An undersea volcano makes a new island in the tropics. When it cools, it and its shores are gradually colonized by life. Corals grow from the shore to a depth of 100 feet or so. So they begin to flourish and form shore reefs.

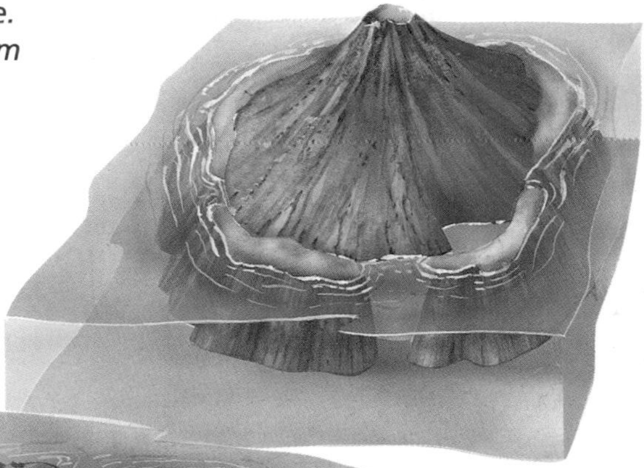

Stage 2
As the island subsides, new corals grow on top of the old reef, fast enough to keep close to the surface. But now only the tip of the island sticks up from the water. This is a barrier reef.

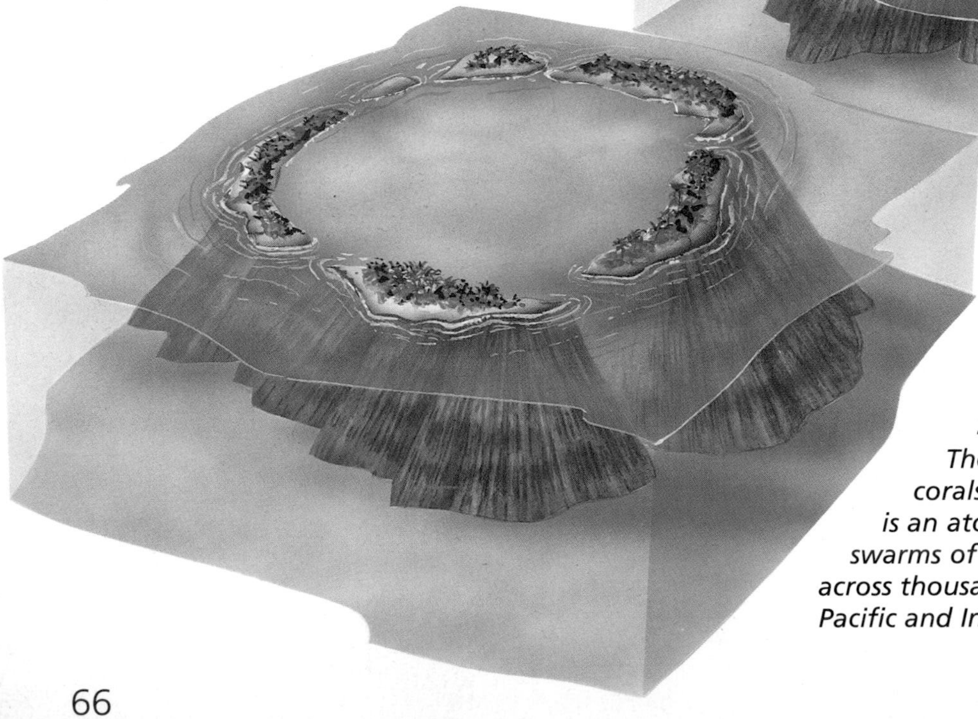

Stage 3
The island sinks completely, but still the corals build on top of the old reef. Now it is an atoll. Coral atolls are markers for whole swarms of sunken, lost islands, which stretch across thousands of miles of sea, in parts of the Pacific and Indian Oceans.

Surviving Earthquakes and Eruptions

People are powerless to stop great natural events such as volcanic eruptions and earthquakes. However, you can be prepared in the case of emergency, and go to a class or demonstration for practical instruction in what to do. If you have to get away, do so fast, since travelling becomes more difficult as roads, trains, and other transport are affected.

Indoors when the quake strikes?
If you are indoors, get away from windows, which might shatter. Shelter under a strong table or desk, or stand in a doorway with the lintel above for protection.

Outdoors when the earth quakes?
Run away from tall buildings, trees, electricity cables, and other high objects, into the most open area you can find. Lie flat in case the tremors throw you off balance.

Volcanic lava
If lava flows near by, get to high ground. Trees or house roofs are not usually safe because lava is heavy—it is liquid rock!—and knocks them over.

Avoid cellars
Do not rush into cellars, subways, or basements if an earthquake occurs. They may get blocked by falling debris, or even collapse and cave in completely.

Volcanic eruption
There may be special shelters in the area, so head for one. Wear thick clothes, a helmet or similar headgear for protection against falling rocks, and a swimming mask, goggles or similar to protect your eyes.

Volcanic fumes
Put a wet scarf, handkerchief, or similar over your nose and mouth, to filter out dust, ash, and fumes.

Amazing Facts

There are about 500 major active volcanoes in the world. Most lie in the "Ring of Fire" around the Pacific Ocean.

The highest volcanic mountain on land is Aconcagua, Argentina, in the Andes Mountains. It is 22,835 feet tall, and extinct.

The tallest active volcano on land is Ojos del Salado, between Chile and Argentina, at 22,600 feet high.

However the tallest volcanic peak is Mauna Kea, Hawaii. From its base on the seabed to its summit is 33,800 feet, with the summit being 13,795 feet above sea level.

Every year 6,000 earthquakes are detected by scientific instruments. Only 30 to 40 cause appreciable damage.

An earthquake in Japan in 1923 caused one area of seabed to drop by 1,300 feet.

An earthquake in Alaska in 1964 caused some parts of the land to rise by 26 feet.

Humans have only recorded history for a few thousand years – the blink of an eye, in terms of the Earth's whole timespan of 4,600 million years. Geological evidence shows that there were periods of huge volcanic eruptions and giant earthquakes in the past, far greater than anything seen in the past 10,000 years.

The highest tsunami (wave caused by seismic events) ever reported was in 1771, in the Ryukyu Islands. It was possibly 280 feet high.

The tallest currently performing geyser is Steamboat Geyser in Yellowstone National Park, Wyoming, USA. It erupts every two or three weeks with plumes up to 330 feet high.

The longest volcanic lava flow is over 40 miles. It erupted from Mount Laki in Iceland, in 1783.

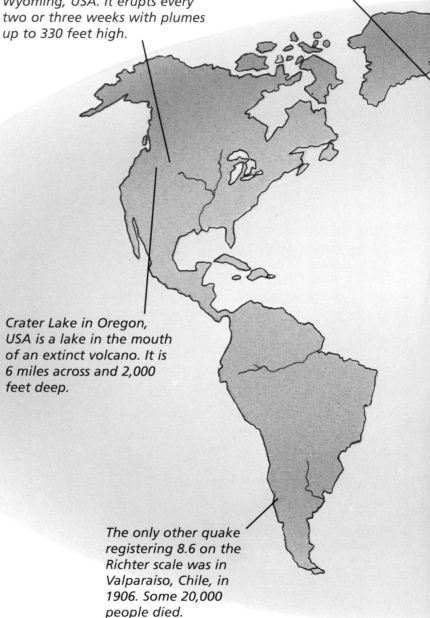

Crater Lake in Oregon, USA is a lake in the mouth of an extinct volcano. It is 6 miles across and 2,000 feet deep.

The only other quake registering 8.6 on the Richter scale was in Valparaiso, Chile, in 1906. Some 20,000 people died.

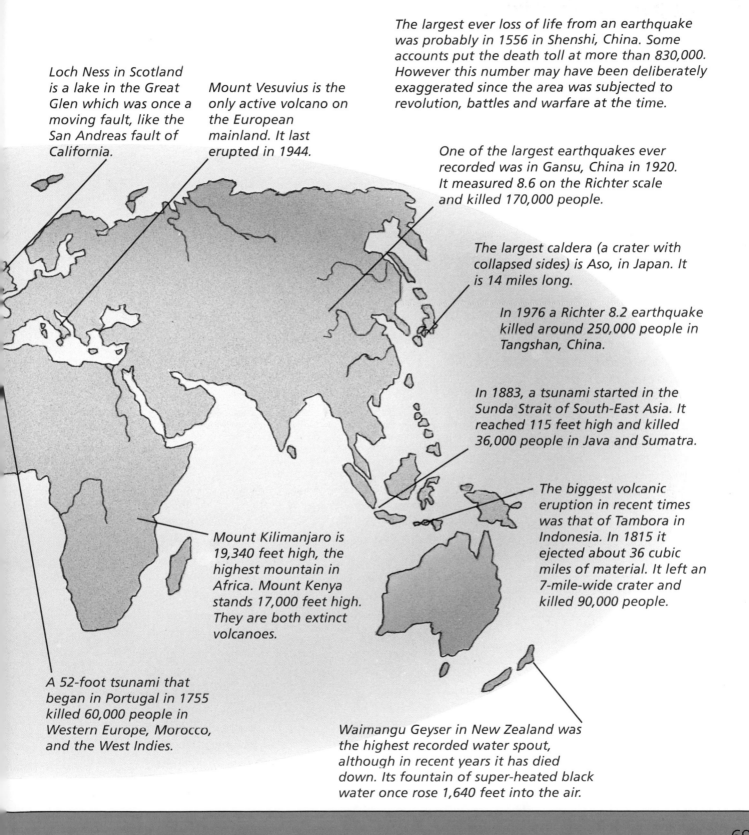

Loch Ness in Scotland is a lake in the Great Glen which was once a moving fault, like the San Andreas fault of California.

Mount Vesuvius is the only active volcano on the European mainland. It last erupted in 1944.

The largest ever loss of life from an earthquake was probably in 1556 in Shenshi, China. Some accounts put the death toll at more than 830,000. However this number may have been deliberately exaggerated since the area was subjected to revolution, battles and warfare at the time.

One of the largest earthquakes ever recorded was in Gansu, China in 1920. It measured 8.6 on the Richter scale and killed 170,000 people.

The largest caldera (a crater with collapsed sides) is Aso, in Japan. It is 14 miles long.

In 1976 a Richter 8.2 earthquake killed around 250,000 people in Tangshan, China.

In 1883, a tsunami started in the Sunda Strait of South-East Asia. It reached 115 feet high and killed 36,000 people in Java and Sumatra.

Mount Kilimanjaro is 19,340 feet high, the highest mountain in Africa. Mount Kenya stands 17,000 feet high. They are both extinct volcanoes.

The biggest volcanic eruption in recent times was that of Tambora in Indonesia. In 1815 it ejected about 36 cubic miles of material. It left an 7-mile-wide crater and killed 90,000 people.

A 52-foot tsunami that began in Portugal in 1755 killed 60,000 people in Western Europe, Morocco, and the West Indies.

Waimangu Geyser in New Zealand was the highest recorded water spout, although in recent years it has died down. Its fountain of super-heated black water once rose 1,640 feet into the air.

Find Out More

The best place to begin your search for more information is your school library. Another excellent source of information is your public library. Most newspapers carry regular reports of new advances in science each week.

For more information about the plants and animals described in this book, check with your nearest natural history museum or wildlife refuge. They can put you in touch with your local natural history associations as well.

We have listed below a selection of books, organizations, videos, and multimedia programs that will help you learn more about EARTHQUAKES AND VOLCANOES.

GENERAL INFORMATION

Center for Environmental Information
  50 West Main
  Rochester, NY 14607
  716-262-2870
National Geographic Society
  17th and M Streets, NW
  Washington, DC 20036
  202-857-7000
National Wildlife Federation
  1400 16th Street NW
  Washington, DC 20036
  202-797-6800

Sierra Club
  100 Bush Street
  San Francisco, CA 94104
  415-291-1600

BOOKS

The Amateur Naturalist Charles C. Watts
  Franklin Watts ISBN 0-531-11002-8
Ecology Projects for Young Scientists
  Martin J. Gutnik
  Franklin Watts ISBN 0-531-04765-2
Exploring Our Living Planet
  Robert D. Ballard,
  National Geographic
  ISBN 0-87044-459-X
Geological Disasters: Earthquakes and Volcanoes Thomas G. Aylesworth
  Franklin Watts
  ISBN 0-531-04488-2
The History of the Earth's Crust
  Don L. Eicher
  Prentice Hall/Simon & Schuster
  ISBN 0-13-389982-9
How Did We Find Out About Earthquakes? Isaac Asimov
  Walker ISBN 0-8027-6306-5
How Did We Find Out About Volcanoes?
  Isaac Asimov
  Walker ISBN 0-8027-6412-6
The Living Planet: A Portrait of the Earth
  David Attenborough
  Little Brown
  ISBN 0-316-05748-7
The New Earth Book: Our Changing Planet Melvin Berger
  Crowell ISBN 0-690-04074-1
The San Francisco Calamity by Earthquake and Fire Charles Morris
  Citadel ISBN 0-8065-0984-8

Science Nature Guides: Fossils
  Thunder Bay Press
  ISBN 1-85028-262-5
Science Nature Guides: Rocks & Minerals
  Thunder Bay Press
  ISBN 1-85028-263-3
Volcano.(Planet Earth Series)
  Time-Life Books
  ISBN 0-8094-4304-X
Volcano: The Eruption and Healing of Mount St. Helens Patricia Lauber
  Bradbury Press ISBN 0-02-754500-8
Volcanoes, Earthquakes, and the Formation of Continents Pierre Kohler
  Barron ISBN 0-8120-3832-0

VIDEOS

National Geographic Society
  produces a wide range of wildlife and geographical videos
Time-Life Video
  produces a wide range of wildlife and geographical videos

MULTIMEDIA

3D Atlas Electronic Arts
The Big Green Disc Gale Research
Eyewitness Encyclopedia of Nature
  Dorling Kindersley
Fourth & Fifth Grade Science
  Sierra Education
Global Learning Mindscape
Multimedia Animals Encyclopedia
  Applied Optical Media
Picture Atlas of the World
  National Geographic Society
Survey of the Animal Kingdom
  Zane Publishing
A World Alive Softline

Glossary

active When a volcano is "alive," erupting or giving out gases, fumes, lava, ash and other substances.

batholith A huge mass of hot, liquid rock that has forced its way between other rocks, and cooled and gone solid, mainly under the surface.

caldera A large bowl-shaped crater, usually formed by volcanic activity.

carnivore An animal that eats other animals, usually a hunter that feeds on meat or flesh.

continental drift The movement of the main continents or landmasses around the surface of the Earth, carried on TECTONIC PLATES.

crust The outermost layer of the Earth, which is mostly solid, and which is very thin compared to the whole Earth (in proportion, it is thinner than the skin on an apple).

dormant When a volcano is quiet or "asleep," but it could become active and erupt at any time.

erode/erosion Wearing away the land by physical methods such as rubbing and scraping, and carrying away the eroded results such as rock particles.

evolution The gradual changes in plants, animals, and other living things over long periods of time, to fit in with and survive in their changing surroundings.

extinct When a volcano has not erupted for a very long time, and it has "died" and will never be active again.

fault A break or fracture in the rocks or ground, where the two sides have moved in relation to each other.

focus The center or place of origin of an earthquake, where the main energy is released as vibrations and movements.

hot-spot A stationary region under the Earth's CRUST which forces up molten rocks and gases so that volcanoes occur there, although the TECTONIC PLATE may slide across it.

herbivore An animal that eats plant food, such as shoots, stems, leaves, buds, flowers, and fruits.

hydrothermal vent A crack or hole, usually on the seabed, through which very hot water gushes from deep below the surface.

lava Rocks and minerals which come out of a volcano and which are so hot that they are melted or molten, so they flow.

lithospheric plate See TECTONIC PLATE.

magma Rocks and minerals which are under the ground and which are so hot that they are melted or molten, so they can flow.

oceanic trench The deepest canyon-like parts of the ocean, where the sea bed plunges almost vertically. It is usually formed as one TECTONIC PLATE subducts (slides) under another.

rift valley A valley formed by cracking and pulling apart of the Earth's CRUST, along a rift or fault.

seismic waves Shock waves of movements and vibrations from an earthquake or similar earth movement.

tectonic plate One of the giant curved plates that makes up the outer surface of the Earth, and which moves or drifts in relation to the other plates. (Also called a lithospheric plate.)

tsunami Large wave and water currents produced by earthquake activity. Sometimes called a "tidal wave," it has nothing to do with tides.

weathering The action of sun, wind, rain, ice and other natural activities that crack and break rocks (see EROSION).

Index